RECESS APPOINTMENTS: AN END-AROUND PRACTICE

RECESS APPOINTMENTS: AN END-AROUND PRACTICE

CHAMBERS Y. NELLS
EDITOR

Novinka Books
An imprint of Nova Science Publishers, Inc.
New York

For permission to use material from this book please contact us:
Telephone 631-231-7269; Fax 631-231-8175
Web Site: http://www.novapublishers.com

Library of Congress Cataloging-in-Publication Data:
Available Upon Request

ISBN: 1-59454-762-9

Published by Nova Science Publishers, Inc. ✦ New York

CONTENTS

PREFACE

Under the Constitution (Article II, Section 2, Clause 2), the President and the Senate share the power to make appointments to high-level policy-making positions in federal departments, agencies, boards, and commissions. Generally, the President nominates individuals to these positions, and the Senate must confirm them before he can appoint them to office. The Constitution also provides an exception to this process. When the Senate is in recess, the President may make a temporary appointment, called a recess appointment, to any such position without Senate approval (Article II, Section 2, Clause 3). This book provides a legal overview of the practice and responses to frequently asked questions.

As reported in chapter 1, article II of the Constitution provides that the President "shall nominate, and by and with the advice and consent of the Senate, shall appoint ambassadors, other public ministers and counsels, judges of the Supreme Court, and all other officers of the United States, whose appointments are not herein otherwise provided for and which shall be established by law." As a supplement to this authority, the Constitution further provides that "[t]he President shall have Power to fill up all Vacancies that may happen during the Recess of the Senate, by granting Commissions which shall expire at the End of their next Session." The Recess Appointments Clause was designed to enable the President to ensure the unfettered operation of the government during periods when the Senate was not in session and therefore unable to perform its advice and consent function.

In addition to fostering administrative continuity, Presidents have exercised authority under the Recess Appointments Clause for political purposes, appointing officials who might have difficulty securing Senate confirmation. Coupled with the ambiguities inherent in interpreting the

Clause, the President's use of the recess appointment power in such a fashion has given rise to significant political and legal controversy since the beginning of the Republic. This report provides an overview of the Clause, with a focus on its historical application and interpretation. This report is a companion piece to CRS Report RL32971, Judicial Recess Appointments: A Legal Overview, by T.J. Halstead (2005), which focuses specifically on the application and interpretation of the Clause in the judicial context.

In chapter 2, Under the Constitution (Article II, Section 2, Clause 2), the President and the Senate share the power to make appointments to high-level policy-making positions in federal departments, agencies, boards, and commissions. Generally, the President nominates individuals to these positions, and the Senate must confirm them before he can appoint them to office. The Constitution also provides an exception to this process. When the Senate is in recess, the President may make a temporary appointment, called a recess appointment, to any such position without Senate approval (Article II, Section 2, Clause 3). This report supplies brief answers to some frequently asked questions regarding recess appointments. It will be updated as events warrant.

In chapter 3, On December 27, 2000, President Bill Clinton used his recess appointment power to place Roger L. Gregory on the Fourth Circuit. The Constitution provides that such appointments "shall expire at the End of their next Session" (in this case, at the end of 2001). This was the first time since President Carter that the recess appointment procedure had been used to select someone to an Article III judgeship, which provides for life tenure and no diminution of salary. The appointment of Gregory raised questions about the meaning of the Recess Clause, Senate prerogatives, and the opportunity of a litigant in federal court to have a case handled by a judge with full independence. On July 20, the Senate confirmed Judge Gregory to a life term.

In: Recess Appointments: An End-Around Practice ISBN 1-59454-762-9
Editor: C.Y.Nells, pp. 1-23

Chapter 1

RECESS APPOINTMENTS: A LEGAL OVERVIEW*

T. J. Halstead

SUMMARY

Article II of the Constitution provides that the President "shall nominate, and by and with the advice and consent of the Senate, shall appoint ambassadors, other public ministers and counsels, judges of the Supreme Court, and all other officers of the United States, whose appointments are not herein otherwise provided for and which shall be established by law." As a supplement to this authority, the Constitution further provides that "[t]he President shall have Power to fill up all Vacancies that may happen during the Recess of the Senate, by granting Commissions which shall expire at the End of their next Session." The Recess Appointments Clause was designed to enable the President to ensure the unfettered operation of the government during periods when the Senate was not in session and therefore unable to perform its advice and consent function.

In addition to fostering administrative continuity, Presidents have exercised authority under the Recess Appointments Clause for political purposes, appointing officials who might have difficulty securing Senate confirmation. Coupled with the ambiguities inherent in interpreting the Clause, the President's use of the recess appointment power in such a fashion has given rise to significant political and legal controversy since the beginning of the Republic. This report provides an overview of the Clause, with a focus on its historical application and interpretation. This report is a companion piece to CRS Report RL32971, Judicial Recess Appointments: A Legal Overview, by T.J. Halstead (2005), which focuses specifically on the application and interpretation of the Clause in the judicial context.

INTRODUCTION

The Constitution establishes that the President "shall nominate, and by and with the advice and consent of the Senate, shall appoint ambassadors, other public ministers and counsels, judges of the Supreme Court, and all other officers of the United States, whose appointments are not herein otherwise provided for and which shall be established by law."[1] As a corollary to this general maxim, the Constitution provides further that "[t]he President shall have Power to fill up all Vacancies that may happen during the Recess of the Senate, by granting Commissions which shall expire at the End of their next Session."[2] The Recess Appointments Clause was adopted by the Constitutional Convention without dissent and without debate regarding the intent and scope of its terms.[3] In Federalist No. 67, Alexander Hamilton refers to the recess appointment power as "nothing more than a supplement...for the purpose of establishing an auxiliary method of appointment, in cases to which the general method was inadequate."[4] During the ratification debates in Pennsylvania, Thomas McKean noted with approval the sharing of the appointive power with the Senate and stated that the Senate need not "be under any necessity of sitting constantly, as has been alleged, for there is an express provision made to enable the President to fill up all vacancies that may happen during their recess; the commissions, to expire at the end of the next session."[5] Likewise, during the ratification debates in North Carolina, Archibald Maclaine stated:

> It has been objected...that the power of appointing officers was something like a monarchical power. Congress are not to be sitting at all times; they

* Excerpted from CRS Report RL33009, dated July 26, 2005.

> will only sit from time to time, as the public business may render it necessary. Therefore the executive ought to make temporary appointments...This power can be vested nowhere but in the executive, because he is perpetually acting for the public; for, though the Senate is to advise him in the appointment of officers, andc., yet, during the recess, the President must do this business, or else it will be neglected; and such neglect may occasion public inconveniences.[6]

In light of its express provisions and these pronouncements, it is generally accepted that the Clause was designed to enable the President to ensure the unfettered operation of the government during periods when the Senate was not in session and therefore unable to perform its advice and consent function.[7] This conception of the recess appointment power as a practical accommodation is supported by the fact that until the Civil War, Congress consistently met for relatively short sessions followed by long recesses of six to nine months.[8] This pattern largely adhered during and after the Civil War, with Congress scheduling an intrasession recess of approximately two weeks from the end of December until the beginning of January.[9] The recess practices of Congress changed in the mid-twentieth century, and are now characterized by more frequent recesses of relatively short duration within sessions of a Congress. Adjournments between sessions are also shorter.[10]

However, in addition to fostering administrative continuity, Presidents have exercised authority under the Recess Appointments Clause for political purposes throughout the history of the republic, giving rise to significant political and legal controversy. For instance, President Madison's recess appointments of Albert Gallatin, John Quincy Adams and James A. Bayard as envoys to negotiate a peace treaty with Great Britain in 1813 prompted heated debate in the Senate.[11] Presidents Jackson, Taylor, and Lincoln made hundreds of recess appointments during their terms.[12] Additionally, recess appointments to the judiciary were common during the early years of the Republic, with the first five Presidents making 31 such appointments, including five to the Supreme Court.[13] Among these, President Washington's recess appointment of John Rutledge as Chief Justice generated significant controversy, ultimately factoring in his rejection by the Senate.[14] It is interesting to note, however, that "no recorded challenge was made to the constitutionality of his recess appointment."[15] In total, twelve Justices have been appointed to the Supreme Court during Senate recesses, and many of these Justices participated in Court business prior to Senate action on their nominations.[16] The mid-nineteenth century phenomena of long congressional adjournments, frequent resort to recess appointments, and the rise of the spoils system in the federal government spurred Congress to impose statutory restrictions on the President's appointment and removal power, including restrictions on paying certain classes of recess appointees.[17] Additionally, the Tenure of Office Act of 1867, that figured prominently in the impeachment effort against President Johnson, included several provisions purporting to limit the recess appointment power of the President.[18]

As noted above, modern congressional recess practices differ significantly from the initial dynamic; sessions of Congress are now characterized by more frequent recesses of relatively short duration and adjournments between sessions have likewise become shorter.[19] Accordingly, controversy over recess appointments may also now adhere to additional factors, such as the length of a recess, and the application of statutory restrictions to recess appointees.

TEXTUAL ISSUES AND HISTORICAL INTERPRETATION

As noted above, practices with respect to recess appointments developed early and debates between Presidents and the Congress over the propriety of particular recess appointments occurred in the formative years of the Republic.[20] Formal consideration of the issue has occurred primarily in the context of Attorney General opinions, with periodic attention from the courts and Congress. Aspects of the recess appointment power were considered as early as 1792, and there were at least nineteen formal Attorneys General opinions in the nineteenth century on recess appointments, the earliest being in 1823. The most recent major exposition by an Attorney General on the recess appointment power was in 1992 and while many of the interpretational questions surrounding the Clause are now deemed, at least by the Executive Branch, to be settled, the course of arriving at these interpretations was not unbroken by contrary opinions and expressions of doubt.

"Vacancies that May Happen"

An initial question that arose was what constitutes a vacancy "that may happen during the Recess of the Senate." If the term "happen" is interpreted as referring only to vacancies that occur during a recess, it necessarily follows that the President would lack authority to make a recess appointment to a vacancy that existed prior to the recess. Conversely, if "happen" is construed more broadly to encompass vacancies that exist during a recess, the President would be empowered to make a recess appointment to any vacant position, irrespective of whether the position became vacant prior to or during "the Recess of the Senate." In 1792, the first Attorney General, Edmund Randolph, responded to an inquiry from Thomas Jefferson, then serving as Secretary of Foreign Affairs, as to whether a recess appointment could be made to the position of Chief Coiner of the Mint, a newly created position for which no nomination had been made before the Senate recessed.[21] Positing whether the unfilled office was a vacancy "which has happened during the recess of the Senate," Randolph concluded that the vacancy occurred on the day the office had been created, and thus could not be filled with a recess appointment.[22] Randolph based his opinion on the text of the Clause and on the "spirit of the Constitution," declaring that the Recess Appointments Clause must be "interpreted strictly" because it serves as "an exception to the general participation of the Senate."[23] In 1799, Alexander Hamilton, then serving as Major General of the Army, responded to a similar inquiry from the Secretary of War, stating "[i]t is clear, that independent of the authority of a special law, the President cannot fill a vacancy which happens during a session of the Senate."[24]

In 1823, Attorney General William Wirt, without mentioning the Randolph interpretation, concluded that the phrase encompassed all vacancies that happen to exist during "the Recess."[25] While Attorney General Wirt acknowledged that the "opposite construction is, perhaps, more strictly consonant with the mere letter" of the Clause (namely, the construction limiting the President to filling vacancies that originate during a recess), he opted for, in his view, "the only construction of the Constitution which is compatible with its spirit, reason, and purpose."[26] Wirt stated further:

> The substantial purpose of the constitution was to keep these offices filled; and powers adequate to this purpose were intended to be conveyed. But if the President shall not have the power to fill a vacancy thus circumstanced, the powers are inadequate to the purpose, and the substance of the Constitution will be sacrificed to a dubious construction of its letter.[27]

Early controversies between the Senate and the President revolved around the meaning of this phrase and opposition to the interpretation offered by Attorney General Wirt had been expressed in the Senate.[28] Story, in his Commentaries on the Constitution, also seems to adopt a construction different from Wirt's at least with respect to newly-created offices to which nominations had not been named (akin to the Randolph position).[29]

Subsequent opinions of the Attorney General in 1832 and 1841 endorsed Wirt's interpretation, although both involved second recess appointments after initial recess commissions had expired, and both opinions noted that, under such circumstances, the vacancy could be said to occur after adjournment of the Senate when the first recess commission ended.[30] Furthermore, Attorney General Taney, in the 1832 opinion stated that the Constitution "was formed for practical purposes, and a construction that defeats the very object of the grant of power cannot be the true one. It was the intention of the constitution that the offices created by law, and necessary to carry on the operations of the government, should always be full, or at all events, that the vacancy should not be a protracted one."[31] Attorney General Taney went on to stress, however, that "vacancies are not *designedly* to be kept open by the President until the recess, for the purpose of avoiding the control of the Senate."[32]

In a brief opinion in 1845, Attorney General Mason concluded that "[i]f vacancies are known to exist during the session of the Senate, and nominations are not then made, they cannot be filled by executive appointments in the recess of the Senate."[33] The Attorney General did not mention his predecessor's opinions to the contrary, although in a subsequent opinion he did note the prior opinions and stated that "[f]rom the commencement of the government, it is believed that a power has been exercised which would appear to be inconsistent with a construction of the section of the constitution which would confine the meaning of the word 'happen' to the time at which the office is in fact vacated."[34] Attorney General Evarts discussed this later opinion of Mason's in an opinion issued in 1868, stating that it "expresses his general concurrence in the construction of the constitutional provision under consideration adopted by his predecessors."[35]

Beginning in 1855, formal Attorneys General opinions returned to the Wirt interpretation, even with respect to newly created offices that had never been filled.[36] Attorney General Bates, in an 1862 opinion, stated that the question "is settled...as far, at least, as a constitutional question can be settled, by the continued practice of your predecessors, and the reiterated opinions of mine, and sanctioned, as far as I know or believe, by the unbroken acquiescence of the Senate."[37] Attorney General Stanberry justified his interpretation by noting that the term vacancy "implies duration, a condition or state of things which may exist for a period of time. Can it be said that the word *happen*, when applied to such a subject, is only properly applicable to its beginning?"[38] Stanberry further stated that executive power must always have capacity for action and that to adopt a narrow construction of the Recess Appointments Clause would interfere with that ability.[39] Attorney General Evarts, in an 1868 opinion, declared the matter so settled that it is "hardly useful to express an opinion as upon an original question."[40] Evarts nonetheless "attempted to weigh anew the opposing interpretation of this clause of the Constitution" in light of the "renewed interest in the whole subject of executive authority in appointments to office, excited by recent legislation of Congress," ultimately concluding that "I...cannot but give my concurrence to the views of my learned predecessors."[41] Subsequent Attorneys General opinions have consistently interpreted "happen" to mean "happen to exist" and have condoned recess appointments to offices that became vacant while the Senate was in session.[42]

This interpretation was first adopted by a federal court in the 1880 decision *In re Farrow*.[43] In *Farrow*, Circuit Justice Woods adopted the reasoning of the aforementioned Attorneys General opinions, stating that "[t]hese opinions exhaust all that can be said on the subject."[44] In reaching his conclusion, Circuit Justice Woods rejected the contrary opinion of a district court, stating that its holding "ought not to be held to outweigh the authority of the great number which are cited in support of the opposite view, and of the practice of the executive department for nearly 60 years, the acquiescence of the senate therein, and the recognition of the power claimed by both houses of congress."[45] The holding in *Farrow* was also followed by Circuit Justice Woods in *In re Yancey*.[46] This interpretation has adhered in judicial opinions considering the issue in the modern era. In *United States v. Allocco*, for instance, the Court of Appeals for the Second Circuit stated that a contrary interpretation "would create executive paralysis and do violence to the orderly functioning of our complex government."[47] Likewise, in *United States v. Woodley*, the Court of Appeals for the Ninth Circuit stated that a contrary interpretation would "lead to the absurd result that all offices vacant on the day the Senate recesses would have to remain vacant at least until the Senate reconvenes."[48] Most recently, in *Evans v. Stephens*, the Court of Appeals for the Eleventh Circuit stated that "interpreting the phrase to prohibit the President from filling a vacancy that comes into being on the last day of a Session but to empower the President to fill a vacancy that arises immediately thereafter (on the first day of a recess) contradicts what we understand to be the purpose of the Recess Appointments Clause: to keep important offices filled and the government functioning."[49] The decisions in *Allocco, Woodley,* and *Evans v. Stephens* are additionally significant, in that all three held that the President's power under the Recess Appointments Clause extends to filling judicial vacancies on Article III courts.[50]

Thus, Attorneys General and courts have rejected a narrow interpretation of the provision and have adopted a construction seen as necessary for continuous and efficient operation of the government. It can also be argued that the Congress has acquiesced in this interpretation, primarily through the passage of statutes, discussed below, that recognize the possibility of such appointments.[51] Furthermore, while congressional statements disputing the prevailing interpretation have been made during periods of controversy surrounding recess appointments, such statements have been made by "individual members of the senate...but not the senate itself."[52]

"The Recess of the Senate"

Another question that emerged later was the meaning of the phrase "the Recess of the Senate" in the Clause. The first formal opinion on the subject was issued by Attorney General Knox in 1901, and concluded that the phrase applied only to adjournments between sessions of Congress (commonly referred to as "intersession" recesses).[53] In reaching this determination, Knox placed significant weight on the use of the definite article "the" in the Recess Appointments Clause, emphasizing that "[i]t will be observed that the phrase is '*the* recess.'"[54] The opinion further concluded that if recess appointments were allowed during periods other than an intersession recess, nothing would prevent an appointment from being made "during any adjournment, as from Thursday or Friday until the following Monday."[55] The opinion specifically rejected a Court of Claims decision that upheld paying the salary of an Army paymaster appointed during a temporary recess in 1867 (the recess extended from July 20 to November 21, 1867).[56]

This position was abandoned in 1921 in an opinion issued by Attorney General Daugherty that declared that an appointment made during a 29 day intrasession recess was constitutional. The Daugherty opinion focused on the practical aspects of the recess appointment dynamic, stating that "[i]f the President's power of appointment is to be defeated because the Senate takes an adjournment to a specified date, the painful and inevitable result will be measurably to prevent the exercise of governmental functions."[57] In support of this interpretation, the Attorney General cited the Court of Claims decision repudiated in the Knox opinion, as well as a 1905 report of the

Senate Judiciary Committee that had been asked to examine the meaning of the term "recess." The report had concluded:

> It was evidently intended by the framers of the Constitution that it [Article II, sec. 2] should mean something real, not something imaginary; something actual, not something fictitious. They used the word as the mass of mankind then understood it and now understand it. It means, in our judgment, in this connection the period of time when the Senate is not sitting in regular or extraordinary session as a branch of the Congress or in extraordinary session for the discharge of executive functions; when its members owe no duty of attendance; when its chamber is empty; when, because of its absence, it can not receive communications from the President or participate as a body in making appointments.... This is essentially a proviso to the provision relative to appointments by and with the advice and consent of the Senate. It was carefully devised so as to accomplish the purpose in view, without in the slightest degree changing the policy of the Constitution, that such appointments are only to be made with the participation of the Senate. Its sole purpose was to render it certain that at all times there should be, whether the Senate was in session or not, an officer for every office, entitled to discharge the duties thereof.[58]

Further emphasizing this functional approach, the Daugherty opinion rejected the notion that this broader interpretation would authorize intrasession appointments during brief adjournments, declaring that "an adjournment for 5 or even 10 days [cannot] be said to constitute the recess intended by the Constitution."[59] The opinion concluded by emphasizing that while "[e]very presumption is to be indulged in favor of the validity of whatever action [the President] may take..., there is a point, necessarily hard of definition, where palpable abuse of discretion might subject his appointment to review."[60] Subsequent Attorney General and Department of Justice Office of Legal Counsel opinions have continued to support the constitutionality of intrasession recess appointments, with more recent pronouncements on the issue asserting that the Clause encompasses all recesses in excess of three days.[61]

It would appear that the pocket veto case, *Kennedy v. Samspon*, has influenced, at least to a minor degree, the view of the propriety of recess appointments during short recesses of the Senate.[62] In *Kennedy*, the court struck down the exercise of the President's pocket veto power during a six-day intrasession recess of the Congress. The Constitution provides that a bill becomes law if not returned by the President after presentment within ten days, "unless the Congress by their adjournment prevent its return, in which case it shall not be a law."[63] The case cast doubt on the validity of all intrasession pocket vetoes, not only those of short duration, and Presidents have since limited their pocket vetoes to periods between sessions or after a Congress has finally adjourned.[64] The Department of Justice, while asserting the validity of a recess appointment during a 33 day intrasession recess, nevertheless advised President Carter that "in view of the functional affinity between the pocket veto and recess appointment powers, Presidents during recent years have been hesitant to make recess appointments during intrasession recesses of the Senate."[65]

While the decision in *Kennedy* appears to have moderated the use of the recess appointment power in some instances, recent Presidents have nonetheless made numerous appointments during short intrasession recesses. President Reagan, for instance, made a number of intrasession recess appointments, one during an 18 day recess ending September 8, 1982, nine during a 23 day recess ending on July 23, 1984, and two during the 13 day recess ending on January 21, 1985. President George H.W. Bush made eight intrasession recess appointments, the shortest occurring during a 17 day recess. President Clinton made numerous intrasession appointments, including five during an 11 day recess ending on January 22, 1996, five during a 16 day recess ending on April 15, 1996, one during a nine day recess ending on June 3, 1996, and one during an 11 day recess ending on January 20, 2001. President George W. Bush has continued the recent practice of making appointments during brief intrasession recesses, including six such appointments during a recess ending on April 28, 2003, four during a 10 day recess ending on April 19, 2004, and, perhaps most controversially, the appointment of William H. Pryor to the Court of Appeals for the Eleventh Circuit on February 20, 2004, on the seventh day of a ten day recess ending on February 23, 2004.[66] The Court of Appeals for the Eleventh Circuit upheld Pryor's appointment, stating:

> The Constitution, on its face, does not establish a minimum time that an authorized break in the Senate must last to give legal force to the President's appointment power under the Recess Appointments Clause. And we do not set that limit today. Although a President has not before appointed a judge to an Article III court during an intrasession recess as short as the one in this case, appointments to other offices — offices ordinarily requiring Senate confirmation — have been made during intrasession recess of about this length or shorter. Furthermore, several times in the past, fairly short intrasession recesses have given rise to presidential appointments of judges to Article III courts.[67]

While it did not specifically address "intrasession" recess appointments, the 1905 Senate Judiciary Committee Report, mentioned above and relied on by Attorney General Daugherty in his 1921 opinion, was prompted by what undoubtedly was the briefest recess ever relied on by a President in order to make recess appointments. At the moment the 58th Congress, 1st session ended at noon, December 7, 1903 and the 2nd session immediately began, President Theodore Roosevelt announced the recess appointment of over 160, mostly military, officers. Two of these appointees had previously held recess appointments and were controversial officeholders. Taking action in accordance with the aforementioned position of Attorney General Knox rejecting the validity of intrasession recess appointments, Roosevelt construed the period between these sessions as a constructive recess.[68] The 1905 Senate Judiciary Committee Report was issued fourteen months after this action and, as is indicated by the quotation included above, emphatically rejected Roosevelt's action. It is important to note, however, that the Report, while expressing disapprobation of the President's exercise of the recess appointment power in such a manner, could be interpreted as validating the execution of intrasession recess appointments generally. Furthermore, Roosevelt's actions could be viewed as a practical manifestation of the potential infirmities of the Knox interpretation: that is to say, if a formalistic interpretation of the Clause rests upon a concern that allowing intrasession appointments will foster systematic avoidance of the Senate's advice and consent function, the fact that a President is able to make such appointments during an instantaneous "constructive recess" of the Senate would appear to belie such a distinction.[69] Alternatively, it could be argued that this historically anomalous event is simply that, and lends no weight to the overall consideration of the matter.

The question of what constituted a recess for purposes of the appointment power arose substantially later than the vacancy issue due to the fact that Congress took few intrasession recesses, other than brief holiday recesses, until the advent of the modern era.[70] Further, as is evident from the aforementioned precedents, the question of what constitutes a "recess" has become more critical as the opportunity for the execution of such appointments has increased. Indeed, as illustrated above, there has been a steady and significant increase in intrasession recess appointments attendant to this shift in the recess practices of the Congress.

Authority and Tenure of Recess Appointees

As a fundamental matter, it is important to note that a confirmed appointee and a recess appointee possess the same legal authority.[71] The commission of a recess appointee expires "at the end of [the Senate's] next session," whereas the service of a confirmed appointee continues until the end of the term or at the pleasure of the President, subject to the requirements laid out by Congress in creating the position.[72] The reconvening of the Senate during the same session after a recess is deemed a continuation of the session and is not regarded as the "next session" within the meaning of the constitutional provision.[73] Thus, for example, persons appointed during the traditional August recess of a 1st session of a Congress could serve until the end of the second session, which would likely be late in the following year. The President may remove a recess appointee before expiration of his term, either by outright removal (assuming he otherwise has discretionary removal authority with respect to the office) or by having another nominee confirmed by the Senate.[74]

If the nomination of the person appointed during the recess is confirmed upon the reconvening of the Senate, it has been held that the new commission for the full statutory term commences from the date of the recess appointment. In other words, the full statutory term relates back to the date on which the person first assumed office by means of the recess appointment. The determination of this question may also depend on the particular statutory provision regarding terms of office and filling of vacancies.[75] It is important to note that Senate rejection of the nomination of a recess appointee does not constitute a removal, and that the rejected nominee may still hold office under the Constitution until the termination of the session.[76] Furthermore, upon the expiration of the constitutional term of a recess appointee, a new recess appointment, either of the same, or another person, may be made.[77] Successive recess appointments of the same individual, however, may implicate the pay restriction delineated in 5 U.S.C. §5503(a)(2), as is discussed in further detail below. Also, while not addressing the issue directly, the court in *Staebler v. Carter* noted that a President "could probably not consistently with the principle of checks and balances grant a recess appointment to one rejected for the particular position by a vote of the Senate."[78]

Additionally, it should be noted that a vacancy must exist before the President can exercise his recess appointment authority.[79] While this observation may seem self evident, the issue may be complicated by the presence of "holdover" provisions that regularly accompany fixed term positions. As an example of such a provision, a member of the Federal Election Commission "may serve on the Commission after the expiration of his or her term until his or her successor has taken office as a member of the Commission."[80] Considering this provision in *Staebler*, the court upheld a recess appointment to a position that was still occupied by a holdover

Federal Election Commissioner, based on a determination that the expiration of the holdover commissioner's formal term created an immediate and ongoing vacancy.[81] Conversely, in *Mackie v. Clinton*, the district court held that the holdover provision for a member of the Board of Governors of the United States Postal Service did not constitute a vacancy sufficient to allow the appointment of a new member pursuant to the Recess Appointments Clause.[82] The relevant statutory provision provides that "[t]he terms of the 9 Governors shall be nine years.... [a] Governor may continue to serve after the expiration of his term until his successor has qualified, but not to exceed one year."[83] Relying on this language, the court invalidated a recess appointment to the Board, based on its determination that the language of the holdover provision established that a holdover Governor was to hold the office after the expiration of his term, for a period not to exceed one year, "unless he dies, resigns, is lawfully removed or 'some successor has qualified,' i.e. has been nominated by the President and confirmed by the Senate."[84] From these decisions, it seems apparent that the issue of whether a holdover provision constitutes a vacancy for recess appointment purposes will hinge on the specific language contained therein.[85]

CONGRESSIONAL ACTION

Since the early history of the Republic, Congress has established a statutory framework designed to protect the Senate's constitutional role in the confirmation process. For instance, the Federal Vacancies Reform Act of 1998 (which governs the filling of vacancies falling outside the scope of the Recess Appointments Clause) establishes which individuals may be designated by the President to temporarily perform the duties and functions of vacant office and the length of time a designee may serve.[86] The original version of the Vacancies Act was enacted in 1868,[87] and the legislative roots of such provisions can be traced back to a 1795 enactment limiting the time a temporary assignee could hold office to six months.[88]

In 1863, Congress attached a rider to the FY1864 Army Appropriations Act that was the forerunner of current statutory provisions. It prohibited the payment of money from the Treasury "to any person acting or assuming to act as an officer, civil, military, or naval, as salary in any office, which is not authorized by some previously existing law, unless where such office shall be subsequently sanctioned by law," and provided further that "nor shall any money be paid out of the Treasury, as a salary, to any person appointed during the recess of the Senate, to fill a vacancy in any existing office, which vacancy existed while the Senate was in session and is by law required to be filled by and with the advice and consent of the Senate, until such appointee shall have been confirmed by the Senate."[89] Under this language, an officer might have to serve without pay (relying on savings or loans), until such time as the Senate consented to the nomination.[90] These provisions were enacted in response to President Lincoln's recess appointment of hundreds of military officers in violation of statutory authorization.[91] The question of the proper interpretation of the word "happen" in the Recess Appointments Clause was raised with several Senators echoing the position of a contemporaneously issued Senate Judiciary Committee Report stating that vacancies that arose while the Senate was in session could not be filled by recess appointment.[92] Other members noted that contrary opinions existed on the subject. Elaborating on the intent of the provision, Senator Fessenden stated:

> "[i]t may not be in our power to prevent the appointment, but it is in our power to prevent the payment; and when payment is prevented, I think that will probably put an end to the habit of making such appointments."[93]

These provisions were followed by the passage of the Tenure of Office Act in 1867, which contained a number of restrictions on the President's appointment and removal powers.[94] Section 2 of the act purported to limit the President's power to suspend officers during a recess to instances where it was determined to the satisfaction of the President that an officer was guilty of misconduct in office, crime, or was incapable or legally disqualified to hold office. Such removals were to be reported to the Senate after it reconvened and, in the event that the Senate did not concur with the suspension, "such officer so suspended" was to "resume the functions of his office."[95] Section 3 of the act purported to limit the President's authority to make recess appointments, providing that such an appointment could be made only if the vacancy occurred by death or resignation. If a recess appointee's nomination was not thereafter confirmed in the next session of the Senate, the office was to "remain in abeyance."[96] The act also delineated criminal penalties and cut-off of salary for violations of its provisions. President Andrew Johnson ignored the provisions of the act in removing Secretary of War Edwin Stanton from office, precipitating his impeachment.[97] Congress amended the act in 1869,[98] and ultimately repealed the provisions entirely in 1887.[99] Similar limits on the President's removal power were struck down as unconstitutional in the 1926 decision of *Myers v. United States*, with the Court stating: "we have no hesitation in holding that... the Tenure of Office Act of 1867, in so far as it attempted to prevent the President from removing executive officers who had been appointed by him by and with the advice and consent of the Senate, was invalid, and that subsequent legislation of the same effect was equally so."[100]

The salary bar for recess appointees that was originally enacted in 1863 remained intact until it was amended in 1940 to provide exceptions to the flat prohibition, making it less burdensome on officeholders.[101] Codified at 5 U.S.C. § 5503, it currently establishes that if a vacancy existed while the Senate was in session a person subsequently appointed to that position during a recess may not receive his salary until he is confirmed by the Senate. Exceptions to this payment prohibition are provided (1) for appointees to vacancies that arise within 30 days of the recess; (2) for appointees to an office for which a nomination was pending at the time of the recess, so long as the nomination is not of an individual appointed during the preceding recess of the Senate; and (3) for appointees selected to an office where a nomination had been made but rejected by the Senate within 30 days of the recess, and the appointee was not the individual so rejected.[102] Section 5503(b) provides that a nomination to fill a vacancy falling within any of the aforementioned exceptions must be submitted to the Senate not later than 40 days after the beginning of the next session of the Senate.

Put more succinctly, a recess appointee to a vacancy existing while the Senate was in session can receive salary pending Senate confirmation of his nomination if (1) the vacancy arose within 30 days before the end of the session, (2) a nomination for the office (other than the nomination of a person appointed during the preceding recess) was pending at the end of the session, or (3) if a nomination for the office was rejected within 30 days of the end of the session and a person other than the rejected nominee receives the recess appointment. These exceptions were designed, as stated in a House Report accompanying the act, "to render the existing prohibition on the payment of salaries more flexible."[103] The report further explained that "[f]rom a practical standpoint it frequently creates difficulties especially in those cases in which a vacancy arose shortly before the close of a congressional session, leaving insufficient time to fill the vacancy by nomination and confirmation. Difficulties also arise in cases in which a session terminates before the Senate acts on pending nominations, as has at times happened."[104]

It is interesting to note that the term "session" as used in § 5503 refers to any time the Senate convenes, and, as such, does not have the same meaning as employed in the Recess Appointment Clause. The version of this law preceding § 5503 used the phrase "termination of the session" as opposed to the phrase "end of the session," which now appears in § 5503(a)(1). This revision was not intended as a substantive change, however.[105] The "termination" phrase was interpreted by the Comptroller General to encompass "any adjournment, whether final or not, in contemplation of a recess covering a substantial period of time."[106]

In addition to the restrictions laid out in § 5503, an annual funding limitation has been included in all Treasury and General Governmental Appropriations Acts for over 60 years that prohibits the payment of any recess appointee whose nomination has been voted down by the Senate.[107]

The provisions governing recess appointments are designed to protect the Senate's advice and consent function by confining the recess appointment power of the President. By targeting the compensation of appointees as opposed to the President's recess appointment power itself, these limitations act as indirect controls on recess appointments, and their constitutionality has not been adjudicated. The court in *Staebler v. Carter* noted in dicta that "if any and all restrictions on the President's recess appointment power, however limited, are prohibited by the Constitution, 5 U.S.C. § 5503...might also be invalid."[108] Additional constitutional concerns might arise from the application of these provisions to judicial recess appointees.[109] Attorneys General have consistently advised Presidents of the applicability of the pay restriction statutes without raising constitutional concerns.[110]

The scope of the decision in *Evans* could be seen as lending credence to the concerns raised in *Staebler*. As touched upon above, the Eleventh Circuit in *Evans* upheld the intrasession recess appointment of William H. Pryor to that court, based upon a broad interpretation of the President's authority under the Clause.[111] The court's decision was accompanied by a dissent from Judge Barkett arguing that a literal and restrictive interpretation of the Clause was necessitated by the "real, concrete concern that the understanding of the recess appointment power embraced by the majority will allow the President to repeatedly bypass the role the Framers intended the Senate to play in reviewing presidential nominees."[112] Accordingly, the majority's acceptance of brief intrasession recess appointments, coupled with the potential constitutional invalidity of the statutory restrictions noted above, could give rise to a dynamic whereby the President would have a legal and constitutional basis upon which to completely bypass the Senate confirmation process, in that the President would be empowered to make successive recess appointments during short recesses with the practical effect of enabling an appointee to serve throughout the course of an Administration without submitting to the Senate confirmation process.[113] The development of such a dynamic is plausible in light of the decisions in *Staebler* and *Evans*, and could arguably transform the Recess Appointments Clause from the supplementary and auxiliary mechanism discussed by Hamilton into a more significant grant of presidential power.

In addition to the aforementioned statutory provisions, Congress has also attempted to influence presidential action in the recess appointment context through resolutions. Resolutions objecting to Madison's appointments of envoys to Great Britain were debated in 1814, but not brought to a vote.[114] It is arguable that a sense of the Senate resolution enacted in 1960 expressing reservation over recess appointments to the Supreme Court has influenced presidential exercise of the recess appointment power in the judicial context.[115] Prompted by President Eisenhower's recess appointments of Earl Warren, William J. Brennan, Jr., and Potter Stewart to the Supreme Court in 1953, 1956, and 1958, respectively, Senator Hart introduced S.Res. 334 to discourage such appointments. The resolution provided that it was the sense of the Senate that this type of recess appointment "is not wholly consistent with the best interests of the Supreme Court, the nominee who may be involved, the litigants before the Court, nor indeed the people of the United States." The resolution further announced the position that such appointments should be avoided "except under unusual and urgent circumstances."[116] No recess appointments to the Supreme Court have been made since the enactment of this resolution, and there has been an attendant decrease in the number of judicial recess appointments generally, with only four such appointments occurring since 1960. However, as is indicated by the decision in *Evans*, the use of the recess appointment power in the judicial context remains a contentious issue.

CONCLUSION

While generally perceived as a straightforward, pragmatic provision designed to foster administrative continuity, the history of the Recess Appointments Clause shows that it has also been employed by Presidents for political purposes throughout the history of the Republic. As such, the Clause has been the source of recurrent controversy, beginning with the Administration of George Washington, and continuing to the current Administration of George W. Bush. Historical interpretation and judicial treatment of the Clause have fleshed out many of its inherent ambiguities, to the extent that there is now precedent supporting the propriety of such appointments irrespective of when the vacancy at issue arose. Likewise, precedent has been established to support recess appointments during both intersession and brief intrasession recesses. However, many tensions remain regarding the proper scope and application of the Clause. These tensions, coupled with the lack of any definitive consideration by the Supreme Court, would thus seem to ensure that the Clause will continue to be the source of political and legal controversy.

REFERENCES

[1] U.S. Const., Art. II, § 2, cl. 2. The appointment of other, so-called "inferior officers," may be vested by Congress in the President alone, courts, or department heads. *Id.*

[2] U.S. Const., Art. II, § 2, cl. 3.

[3] Louis Fisher, *Recess Appointments of Federal Judges*, Congressional Research Service, Rep. No. CRS Report RL31112 at 1 (2001).

[4] *The Federalist, No. 67*, at 409-10 (Alexander Hamilton) (Clinton Rossiter ed. 1961).

[5] 2 *The Documentary History of the Ratification of the Constitution* 537 (Merrill Jensen, ed. 1976).

[6] Edward A Hartnett, *Recess Appointments of Article III Judges: Three Constitutional Questions*, 26 Cardozo L. Rev. 377, 380-81 (2005) (quoting 4 *The Founders' Constitution* 37, 102-03 (P. Kurland ed., 1787)).

[7] Henry B. Hogue, *Recess Appointments: Frequently Asked Questions*, Congressional Research Service, Rep. No. CRS Report RS21308 at 1 (2005).

[8] *Id. See also* Michael A. Carrier, *When is the Senate in Recess for Purposes of the Recess Appointments Clause?* 92 Mich. L. Rev. 2204, 2212 (1994).

[9] *Id.* at 2212.

[10] *See* Michael B. Rappaport, *The Original Meaning of the Recess Appointments Clause*, 52 UCLA L. Rev. 1487, 1500-01 (2005).

[11] *See*, 20 Op. A.G. 284 (1996).

[12] *See*, Fish, Carl R. "Removal of Officials by the Presidents of the United States." Annual Report of the American Historical Association

for the Year 1899. Vol. 1. Washington, D.C., Government Printing Office (1900).

[13] Thomas A Curtis, *Recess Appointments to Article III Courts: The Use of Historical Practice in Constitutional Interpretation*, 84 Colum. L. Rev. 1758, 1755 (1984).

[14] *Id.* at 1775-76.

[15] *Id.* at 1776.

[16] Henry B. Hogue, *The Law: Recess Appointments to Article III Courts*, Presidential Studies Quarterly 34, No. 3 at 661 (2004).

[17] *See* n.89 and accompanying text, *infra.*

[18] *See* n.94 and accompanying text, *infra.*

[19] Rappaport, n.10, *supra.*

[20] *See* Curtis, n.13, *supra*, at 1758.

[21] Edmund Randolph, Opinion on Recess Appointments (July 7, 1792), in 24 The Papers of Thomas Jefferson, at 165-67 (John Catanzariti et al. Ed., 1990). *See also*, Hartnett, n.6, *supra*, at 384-86; Rappaport, n.10, *supra*, at 1518-19.

[22] Randolph, n.21, *supra*, at 166; Rappaport, n.10, *supra*, at 1519.

[23] Randolph, n.21, *supra*, at 166; Rappaport, n.10, *supra*, at 1519.

[24] Rappaport, n.10, *supra*, at 1519.

[25] 1 Op. A.G. 631, 633-34 (1823).

[26] *Id.*

[27] *Id.* at 632.

[28] *See* George H. Haynes, *The Senate of the United States*, Vol. 2 at 772-73 (Russell and Russell ed., 1960).

[29] 3 Story, Commentaries on the Constitution of the United States 411 (Da Capo ed., 1970).

[30] 2 Op. A.G. 525 (1832); 3 Op. A.G. 673 (1841).

[31] 2 Op. A.G. at 526-27.

[32] 2 Op. A.G. at 528 (emphasis in original).

[33] 4 Op. A.G. 361, 363 (1845).

[34] 4 Op. A.G. 523, 525 (1846).

[35] 12 Op. A.G. 455 (1868).

[36] 7 Op. A.G. 186 (1855); 18 Op. A.G. 28 (1884); 19 Op. A.G. 261 (1889).

[37] 10 Op. A.G. 356 (1862)

[38] 12 op. A.G. 32, 34 (1866) (emphasis in original).

[39] *Id.* at 38.

[40] 12 Op. A.G. 449, 452 (1868).

[41] *d.*

[42] *See* 14 Op. A.G. 562 (1875); 15 Op. A.G. 207 (1877); 16 Op. A.G. 522 (1880); 16 Op. A.G. 538 (1880); 17 Op. A.G. 521 (1883); 18 Op. A.G. 29 (1884); 19 Op. A.G. 261 (1889); 26 Op. A.G. 234 (1907); 30 Op. A.G. 314 (1914); 33 Op. A.G. 20 (1921); 41 Op. A.G. 463 (1960); 6 U.S. Op. Off. Legal Counsel 585 (1982).

[43] 3 Fed. 112, 116 (C.C.N.D. Ga. 1880) (stating that the President has the power to make appointments "notwithstanding the fact that the vacancy filled by his appointment first happened when the senate was in session.").

[44] *Id.* at 115.

[45] *Id.* at 115 (rejecting the holding in *Case of District Attorney of United States*, 7 Fed. Cas. 731 (No. 3924, E.D. Pa. 1868)); *see also*, contrary opinion in *Schenck v. Peay*, 21 Fed. Cas. 672 (No. 12451 E.D. Ark. 1869).

[46] 28 Fed. 445, 450 (C.C.W.D. Tenn. 1886).

[47] 305 F.3d 704, 712 (2d Cir. 1962), *cert. denied*, 371 U.S. 964 (1963).

[48] 751 F.2d 1008, 1012 (9th Cir. 1985), *cert. denied*, 475 U.S. 1048 (1986).

[49] 387 F.3d 1220, 1226-27 (11th Cir. 2004), *cert. denied*, 125 S.Ct. 1640 (2005).

[50] For an analysis of the interplay of the Recess Appointments Clause and Article III of the Constitution, *see* CRS Report RL32971, *Judicial Recess Appointments: A Legal Overview*, by T.J. Halstead (2005).

[51] *See* n.89 and accompanying text, *infra*.

[52] *Farrow*, 3 Fed. at 115.

[53] 23 Op. A.G. 599 (1901).

[54] 23 Op. A.G. at 600 (emphasis in original).

[55] *Id.* at 603.

[56] *See Gould v. United States*, 19 Ct. Cl. 593 (1884).

[57] 33 Op. A.G. 20, 23 (1921).

[58] S.Rept. No. 4389, 58th Cong., 3d Sess. 2 (1905); 39 Cong. Rec. 3823-24 (1905).

[59] *Id.* at 25.

[60] *Id.* at 25.

[61] *See Evans v. Stephens*, No. 04-828, Brief for the United States in Opposition to Petition for a Writ of Certiorari, at 11 (U.S. 2005); *Mackie v. Clinton*, Memorandum of Points and Authorities in support of Defendants' Opposition to Plaintiffs' Motion for Partial Summary Judgment, at 24-26, Civ. Action No. 93-0032-LFO (D.D.C. 1993).

[62] 511 F.2d 430 (D.C. Cir. 1974).

[63] U.S. Const., Art. I, § 7, cl. 2.

[64] See *Barnes v. Kline*, 759 F.2d 21 (D.C. Cir. 1985) (invalidating intersession pocket veto), *vacated as moot sub nom., Burke v. Barnes*, 479 U.S. 361 (1987).

[65] 3 U.S. Op. Off. Legal Counsel 314, 316 (1979).

[66] Information on recess appointments may be obtained in the *Weekly Compilation of Presidential Documents*.

[67] *Evans v. Stephens*, 387 F.3d 1220 (11th Cir. 2004), *cert. denied*, 125 S.Ct. 16401 (2005).

[68] *See* Hogue, n.16, *supra*, at 671.

[69] *See* Hartnett, n.6, *supra*, at 416.

[70] *See* Carrier, n.8, *supra*, at 2212-13.

[71] *See* Hogue, n.7, *supra*, at 3.

[72] *Id.* at 3.

[73] 41 Op. A.G. 463, 470-71 (1960); 28 Comp. Gen. 121 (1948).

[74] 41 Op. A.G. at 471.

[75] 37 Op. A.G. 282 (1933); 9 Comp. Gen. 190 (1929).

[76] *See, In re Marshalship*, 20 Fed. 379 (D. Ala. 1884); 2 Op. A.G. 336 (1830); 21 Comp. Dec. 789 (1915) (Comptroller of the Currency).

[77] 2 Op. A.G. 525 (1832); 3 Op. A.G. 673 (1841); 4 Op. A.G. 523 (1846); 11 Op. A.G. 179 (1865); 28 Comp. Gen. 30, 38 (1948); 28 Comp. Gen. 121, 129 (1948).

[78] 464 F.Supp. at 601, n.41.

[79] *See* 3 U.S. Op. Off. Legal Counsel 314, 317 (1979) ("A recess appointment presupposes the existence of a vacancy. If there is an incumbent in the office the recess appointment in itself does not effect a removal of the incumbent so as to create a vacancy. Before the President can exercise his recess appointment power in such a case he must exercise his constitutional removal power to the extent it is available, or, if not available, the incumbent must resign" (citations omitted)).

[80] 2 U.S.C. §437c(a)(2)(B).

[81] 464 F.Supp. at 589.

[82] 827 F.Supp. 56 (1993), *vacated as moot*, 1994 WL 163761 (D.C. Cir. 1994).

[83] 39 U.S.C. §202(b).

[84] *Mackie*, 827 F.Supp. at 58. *See also*, *Swan v. Clinton*, 100 F.3d 973 (D.C. Cir. 1996); *Wilkinson v. Legal Services Corp.*, 80 F.Supp. 891 (D.D.C. 1994), *reversed on other grounds*, *Wilkinson v. Legal Services Corp.*, 80 F.3d 535 (D.C. Cir. 1996); *McCalpin v. Dana*, No. 85-542

(D.D.C. 1982), *vacated as moot sub nom., McCalpin v. Durant*, 766 F.2d 535 (D.C. Cir. 1985).

[85] *See* Hogue, n.7, *supra*, at 3; Fisher, n.3, *supra*, at 8.

[86] 5 U.S.C. §§ 3345-3349d. The Vacancies Act provides the exclusive means for authorizing the temporary filling of advice and consent positions unless otherwise expressly provided in law, or unless the President exercises his authority under the Recess Appointments Clause.

[87] 15 Stat. 168 (1868).

[88] 1 Stat. 415 (1795).

[89] 12 Stat. 642, 646 (1863).

[90] *See* Fisher, n.3, *supra*. at 5.

[91] *See* 33 Cong. Globe 564-65 (1863).

[92] S. Rep. No. 80, 37th Cong., 3d Sess. (1863).

[93] 33 Cong. Globe 565 (1863).

[94] 14 Stat. 430 (1867).

[95] *Id.*

[96] *Id.* at 431.

[97] *See* Jonathan Turley, *Senate Trials and Factional Disputes: Impeachment as a Madisonian Device*, 40 Duke L.J. 1, 87-88 (1999).

[98] 16 Stat. 6 (1869).

[99] 24 Stat. 500 (1887).

[100] 272 U.S. 52, 176 (1926).

[101] *See* Fisher, n.3, *supra*, at 6.

[102] 5 U.S.C. § 5503(a)(1)-(3).

[103] H. Rep. No. 2646, 76th Cong., 3d Sess. 1 (1940).

[104] *Id. See also*, 28 Comp. Gen. 30 (1948)

[105] *See* S. Rep. No. 1380, 89th Cong., 2d Sess. 20, 105 (1966).

[106] 28 Comp. Gen. 30, 37 (1948); *see also* 41 Op. A.G.463, 473-75 (1960)

[107] *See, e.g.*, P.L. 108-447, Div. H, Sec. 609; 118 Stat. 3274.

[108] 464 F.Supp. 585, 596 (D.D.C. 1979).

[109] *See* Halstead, n.50, *supra*, at 11.

[110] *See, e.g.,* 15 U.S. Op. Off. Legal Counsel 91 (1991); 41 Op. A.G. 463, 472-80 (1960).

[111] *See* Halstead, n.50, *supra*, at 8-11.

[112] *Evans*, 387 F.3d at 1235.

[113] *See* Halstead, n.50, *supra*, at 11for additional consideration of this issue in the Article III context.

[114] *See* Haynes, n.28, *supra*, at 772-73.

[115] 106 Cong. Rec. 18145 (1960).

[116] 106 Cong. Rec. 12761 (1960). *See also*, Fisher n.3, *supra*, at 16.

In: Recess Appointments: An End-Around Practice ISBN 1-59454-762-9
Editor: C.Y.Nells, pp. 25-34

Chapter 2

RECESS APPOINTMENTS: FREQUENTLY ASKED QUESTIONS*

Henry B. Hogue

SUMMARY

Under the Constitution (Article II, Section 2, Clause 2), the President and the Senate share the power to make appointments to high-level policy-making positions in federal departments, agencies, boards, and commissions. Generally, the President nominates individuals to these positions, and the Senate must confirm them before he can appoint them to office. The Constitution also provides an exception to this process. When the Senate is in recess, the President may make a temporary appointment, called a recess appointment, to any such position without Senate approval (Article II, Section 2, Clause 3). This report supplies brief answers to some frequently asked questions regarding recess appointments. It will be updated as events warrant.

---

* Excerpted from CRS Report RS21308, dated March 15, 2005.

What is the Purpose of a Recess Appointment?

The Constitution states that "[t]he President shall have Power to fill up all Vacancies that may happen during the Recess of the Senate, by granting Commissions which shall expire at the End of their next Session" (Article 2, Section 2, Clause 3). The records of debate at the Constitutional Convention and the Federalist Papers provide little evidence of the framers' intentions in the recess appointment clause. Opinions by later Attorneys General, however, suggested that the clause was meant to allow the President to maintain the continuity of administrative government through the temporary filling of offices during periods when the Senate was not in session, at which time his nominees could not be considered or confirmed.[1] This interpretation is bolstered by the fact that both Houses of Congress had relatively short sessions and long recesses during the early years of the Republic. In fact, until the beginning of the 20th century, Congress was, on average, in session less than half the year. Throughout the history of the republic, Presidents have also sometimes used the recess appointment power for political reasons. For example, recess appointments enable the President to temporarily install an appointee who probably would not be confirmed by the Senate.

How Often have Recent Presidents Made Recess Appointments?

During his two terms in office, President Ronald W. Reagan made 240 recess appointments, of which 116 were to full-time positions. President George H. W. Bush made 77 recess appointments during his term of office; 18 were to full-time positions. President William J. Clinton made 140 recess appointments during his eight years in office, 95 to full-time positions. During his first term in office, President George W. Bush made 110 recess appointments, of which 66 were to full-time positions.

How Long does a Recess Appointment Last?

A recess appointment expires at the end of the Senate's next session or when an individual (either the recess appointee or someone else) is nominated, confirmed, and permanently appointed to the position, whichever occurs first. In practice, this means that a recess appointment may last for up to nearly two years. If the President makes a recess appointment between sessions or between Congresses, that appointment will expire at the end of the following session. If he makes the appointment during a recess in the middle of a session, that appointment also will expire at the end of the following session. In this case, the duration of the appointment will include the balance of the session in progress plus the full length of the session that follows.

Two recess appointments by President George W. Bush provide examples. On January 16, 2004, during the recess between the first and second sessions of the 108th Congress, President Bush recess-appointed Charles W. Pickering to the U.S. Court of Appeals for the Fifth Circuit. Pickering's appointment expired on December 8, 2004, at the end of the second session of the 108th Congress. Several weeks after the Pickering appointment, on February 20, 2004, President Bush recess-appointed William H. Pryor to the U.S. Court of Appeals for the Eleventh Circuit. This recess appointment took place during a 10-day adjournment of the Senate within the second session of the 108th Congress. Consequently, Pryor's recess appointment expires at the end of the first session of the 109th Congress, which is likely to occur in the last quarter of 2005. Although the Pickering and Pryor recess appointments were only several weeks apart, Pryor may serve a year longer because his appointment was made during an intrasession recess.

The meaning of the phrase "End of their [the Senate's] next session" in the Constitution's recess appointment clause is not precisely defined. A Senate session is usually considered to end at the time of *sine die* adjournment. The Senate could, however, be called back into session after *sine die* adjournment if certain conditions have been included in the adjournment resolution. Nonetheless, *sine die* adjournment is generally considered to be the end of the Senate's session for purposes of the expiration of a recess appointment.[2]

FOR THE PURPOSES OF RECESS APPOINTMENTS, WHAT CONSTITUTES A VACANCY?

The wording of the constitutional provision allowing recess appointments leads to a question about which positions could actually be filled that way. The question revolves around the phrase "Vacancies that may happen during the Recess of the Senate." Does "happen" mean "happen to exist" or "happen to occur"? The first meaning would allow the President to make recess appointments to any position that becomes vacant prior to the recess and continues to be vacant during the recess, as well as positions that become vacant during the recess. The second meaning would allow recess appointments only to positions that become vacant during the recess. Although this question was a source of controversy in the early nineteenth century, Attorneys General and courts have now long supported the first, broader interpretation of the phrase.

A second question regarding the meaning of "Vacancies" arises in connection with recess appointments to fixed term positions, such as those often associated with regulatory boards and commissions. In order to promote continuity of operations, Congress has often included "holdover" provisions in the statutory language creating such positions. The question then arises whether or not a position is vacant, for the purposes of a recess appointment, if an individual is continuing to serve, under a holdover provision, past the end of his or her term. The courts have varied in their rulings on this matter, and it has not been settled definitively by an appellate court. Based on decisions to date, however, the answer appears to hinge on the specific language of the holdover provision. For example, if the language is mandatory (the officeholder "*shall* continue to serve after the expiration of his term"), rather than permissive ("*may* continue to serve"), the position has been seen by the courts as not vacant, and therefore not available for a recess appointment.[3] When the provision includes a specific time limit for the holdover, such as one year, the position has also been seen as not vacant.[4]

What is the Difference between the Authority of a Confirmed Appointee and that of a Recess Appointee?

Both carry the same legal authority. The principal difference is the potential length of the appointment. The recess appointment is temporary (see above) and the confirmed appointment continues until the end of the term or at the pleasure of the President, depending on the statutory provisions creating the position.

Does the Recess Appointee Receive the Same Rate of Pay as the Person Vacating the Position?

Yes. However, two provisions of law may prevent a recess appointee from being paid under certain circumstances. (See below, "Are there any legal constraints on the President's recess appointment power?")

How Long Must the Senate be in Recess before a President may Make a Recess Appointment?

The Constitution does not specify the length of time that the Senate must be in recess before the President may make a recess appointment. Over the last century, as shorter recesses have become more commonplace, Attorneys General and Offices of Legal Counsel have offered differing views on this issue. Most recently, in 1993, a Department of Justice brief implied that the President may make a recess appointment during a recess of more than three days.[5] Appointments made during short recesses (less than 30 days), however, have sometimes aroused controversy, and they may involve a political cost for the President. Controversy has been particularly acute in instances where Senators perceive that the President is using the recess appointment process to circumvent the confirmation process for a nominee who is opposed in the Senate. Although President Theodore Roosevelt once made recess appointments during an intersession recess of less than one day, the shortest length of a recess during which appointments have been made during the past 20 years was 10 days.

Are there any Legal Constraints on the President's Recess Appointment Power?

There is no qualification to the President's "Power to fill up all Vacancies..." in the constitutional provision. Neither is there a statutory constraint on this power. There are, however, two points of statutory law that may prevent a recess appointee from being paid. Under 5 U.S.C. 5503(a), if the position to which the President makes a recess appointment fell vacant while the Senate was in session, the recess appointee may not be paid from the Treasury until he or she is confirmed by the Senate. The salary prohibition does not apply: (1) if the vacancy arose within 30 days before the end of the session; (2) if a nomination for the office (other than the nomination of someone given a recess appointment during the preceding recess) was pending when the Senate recessed; or (3) if a nomination was rejected within 30 days before the end of the session and another individual was given the recess appointment. A recess appointment falling under any one of these three exceptions must be followed by a nomination to the position not later than 40 days after the beginning of the next session of the Senate.[6] For this reason, when a recess appointment is made, the President generally submits a new nomination to the position even when an old nomination is pending. In addition, although recess appointees whose nominations to a full term are subsequently rejected by the Senate may continue to serve until the end of their recess appointment, a provision of the Transportation, Treasury, Independent Agencies, and General Government Appropriations Act may prevent them from being paid after their rejection. (See below, "What happens if the nomination of someone holding a recess appointment is rejected by the Senate?")

Is there any Difference between Recess Appointments Made between Sessions and those Made During a Recess within a Session?

Recent Presidents have made both *intersession* (between sessions or Congresses) and *intrasession* (during a recess within a session) recess appointments. Intrasession recess appointments were rare, however, prior to the 1940s.[7] Intrasession recess appointments have sometimes provoked controversy in the Senate, and there is also an academic literature that has drawn their legitimacy into question.[8] Intrasession recess appointments are usually of longer duration than intersession recess appointments. (See above, "How long does a recess appointment last?")

Does a Recess Appointee have to be Nominated to the Position as Well?

The President is not required to nominate the recess appointee to the appointed position. The President will sometimes use a recess appointment to fill a position while a different nominee to the same position is going through the confirmation process in the Senate. Under certain conditions, however, a provision of law may prevent a recess appointee from being paid from the Treasury if he or she has not been nominated to the position. (See above, "Are there any legal constraints on the President's recess appointment power?")

What Happens if the Nomination of Someone Holding a Recess Appointment is Rejected by the Senate?

Rejection by the Senate does not end the recess appointment. Payment to the appointee may be prevented, however, by a recurring provision of the Transportation, Treasury, Independent Agencies, and General Government Appropriations Act. The provision reads, "No part of any appropriation for the current fiscal year contained in this or any other Act shall be paid to any person for the filling of any position for which he or she has been nominated after the Senate has voted not to approve the nomination of said person."[9] This provision has been part of this annual funding activity for at least 50 years. As a practical matter, nominations are rarely rejected by a vote of the full Senate.

Can the President Make Successive Recess Appointments to the Same Position?

The President may make successive recess appointments of the same or a different individual to a position. Payment from the Treasury to the appointee may be limited, however, under 5 U.S.C. 5503. (See also above, "Are there any legal constraints on the President's recess appointment power?") Subsection 5503(a) provides, in part, that:

> Payment for services may not be made from the Treasury of the United States to an individual appointed during a recess of the Senate to fill a vacancy in an existing office, if the vacancy existed while the Senate was in session and was by law required to be filled by and with the advice and consent of the Senate, until the appointee has been confirmed by the Senate.

The provision allows three exemptions to this pay prohibition, two of which would not apply in this situation. Under the remaining exemption, "if, at the end of the session, a nomination for the office, other than the nomination of an individual appointed during the preceding recess of the Senate, was pending before the Senate for its advice and consent," the prohibition would not apply.[10] The clause "other than the nomination of an individual appointed during the preceding recess of the Senate" probably would prevent payment in the case of most successive recess appointments. This interpretation has been supported by the Office of Legal Counsel (OLC), Department of Justice, which stated in 1991, "Although its language is far from clear, section 5503(a) has been interpreted as prohibiting the payment of compensation to successive recess appointees."[11]

CAN A RECESS APPOINTMENT BE USED TO FILL A VACANCY ON THE FEDERAL BENCH?

Presidents have long made recess appointments to the federal judiciary. In recent years, however, recess appointments of federal judges have been unusual and controversial. Over the past 20 years, there have been only three recess appointments to fill Article III judgeships. President William J. Clinton named Roger L. Gregory to the Fourth Circuit on December 27, 2000 as a recess appointment, a step that was met by some opposition in the Senate. Ultimately, Gregory was re-nominated by President George W. Bush and confirmed by the Senate. On January 16, 2004, President George W. Bush recess-appointed Charles W. Pickering to the U.S. Court of Appeals for the Fifth Circuit. Pickering's appointment expired on December 8, 2004, at the end of the second session of the 108th Congress, and he retired.[12] On February 20, 2004, President Bush named William H. Pryor to the Eleventh Circuit Court of Appeals. Pryor's recess appointment expires at the end of the first session of the 109th Congress.[13]

REFERENCES

[1] An opinion by Attorney General William Wirt in 1823 concerning the meaning of the word "happen" in the clause. In part, he stated, "The substantial purpose of the constitution was to keep these offices filled; and the powers adequate to this purpose were intended to be conveyed." 1 Op. A.G. at 632.

[2] See, for example, 41 Op. A.G. 463 (1960), which, in the context of a discussion of the expiration of recess appointments, refers to *sine die* adjournment as the end of the Senate's session.

[3] Compare *Staebler v. Carter*, 464 F. Supp. 585 (1979), and *Wilkinson v. L.S.C.*, 865 F. Supp. 891 (1994).

[4] See *Mackie v. Clinton*, 827 F. Supp. 56 (1993).

[5] *Mackie v. Clinton*, Civil Action 93-0032-LFO, July 2, 1993.

[6] Congress placed limits on payments to recess appointees as far back as 1863. The current provisions date from 1940 (ch. 580, 54 Stat. 751, 5 U.S.C. 56, revised, and recodified at 5 U.S.C. 5503, by P.L. 89-554, 80 Stat. 475). For a legal history and overview of recess appointments, see CRS Report 87-832 A, *Recess Appointments: Legal Overview,* by Richard C. Ehlke (archived; contact author for more information).

[7] Prior to 1943, only Presidents Andrew Johnson, Warren G. Harding, and Calvin Coolidge had made such appointments. Johnson appointed 14 individuals during a single intrasession recess, and Harding and Coolidge each appointed one person in this way.

[8] Regarding Senate controversy, see Sen. George Mitchell, "The Senate's Constitutional Authority to Advise and Consent to the Appointment of Federal Officers," *Congressional Record*, vol. 139, July 1, 1993, p. 15266; and Senate Legal Council, "Memorandum of United States Senate as Amicus Curiae in Support of Plantiffs' Motion, and in Opposition to Defendants' Motions, for Summary Judgment on Count Two," U.S. District Court for the District of Columbia, *Mackie v. Clinton*, C.A. No. 93-0032-LFO, *Congressional Record*, vol. 139, July 1, 1993, pp. 15267-15274. For academic literature, see, for example, Michael A. Carrier, "When Is the Senate in Recess for Purposes of the Recess Appointments Clause?" *Michigan Law Review*, vol. 92, June 1994.

[9] P.L. 108-447, Div. H, Sec. 609; 118 Stat. 3274.

[10] 5 U.S.C. 5503(a)(2).

[11] 15 Op. O.L.C. 93 (1991). See also 6 Op. O.L.C. 585 (1982); 41 Op. A.G. 463 (1960).

[12] Adam Liptak, "Judge Appointed by Bush After Impasse in Senate Retires," *The New York Times*, Dec. 10, 2004, p. A20.

[13] For more see CRS Report RL31112, *Recess Appointments of Federal Judges*, by Louis Fisher; and CRS Report RS22039, *Federal Recess Judges*, by Louis Fisher.

In: Recess Appointments: An End-Around Practice ISBN 1-59454-762-9
Editor: C.Y.Nells, pp. 35-66

Chapter 3

RECESS APPOINTMENTS OF FEDERAL JUDGES*

Louis Fisher

SUMMARY

On December 27, 2000, President Bill Clinton used his recess appointment power to place Roger L. Gregory on the Fourth Circuit. The Constitution provides that such appointments "shall expire at the End of their next Session" (in this case, at the end of 2001). This was the first time since President Carter that the recess appointment procedure had been used to select someone to an Article III judgeship, which provides for life tenure and no diminution of salary. The appointment of Gregory raised questions about the meaning of the Recess Clause, Senate prerogatives, and the opportunity of a litigant in federal court to have a case handled by a judge with full independence. On July 20, the Senate confirmed Judge Gregory to a life term.

On December 27, 2000, President Bill Clinton used his recess appointment power to place Roger L. Gregory on the Fourth Circuit. The Constitution provides that such appointments "shall expire at the End of their next Session" (in this case, at the end of 2001). This was the first time since

President Carter that the recess appointment procedure had been used to select someone to an Article III judgeship. The appointment of Gregory raised questions about the meaning of the Recess Clause, Senate prerogatives, and the opportunity of a litigant in federal court to have a case handled by a judge with full independence.

The recess appointment power has been used in some instances for non–Article III judges. Judges on Article III, or constitutional, courts are entitled to lifetime tenures and are protected against diminution of their salaries. Those privileges do not extend to non–Article III courts (also called Article I or legislative courts). Over the past two centuries, Article I courts have included territorial courts, legislative courts, military courts, U.S. magistrates, and, at various times, the courts of the District of Columbia. On December 10, 1997, President Clinton used his recess appointment power to place Christine Odell Cook Miller on the U.S. Court of Federal Claims, which is an Article I court because the judges have 15-year terms. Similarly, on January 19, 2001, President Clinton selected Sarah L. Wilson as a recess appointee to the same court. This report focuses on recess appointments of Article III judges.

RECESS CLAUSE

The Constitution gives the President the power to nominate, "and by and with the Advice and Consent of the Senate," appoint ambassadors, other public ministers and consuls, Justices of the Supreme Court, and "all other Officers of the United States, whose Appointments are not herein otherwise provided for, and which shall be established by Law." The President also has power "to fill up all Vacancies that may happen during the Recess of the Senate, by granting Commissions which shall expire at the End of their next Session."[1]

The framers recognized that the Senate would not always be in session to give advice and consent to presidential nominations. To cover these periods, the President is authorized to make recess appointments that are needed to keep government operating effectively. This provision was adopted at the Constitutional Convention without a dissenting vote and with virtually no record to fix its intent and scope.[2] The power to make recess appointments is stated in general terms, with no distinctions between its application to judges or non-judges. However, there is a tension between the

* Excerpted from CRS Report RL31112, dated September 2, 2001.

appointment of recess judges—serving on a temporary basis—and the general principle of judicial independence assured by lifetime tenure.

Federalist No. 67, written by Alexander Hamilton, adds little to the intent of the Recess Clause.[3] He states that the "general mode" of appointing officers of the United States required joint action by the President and the Senate, and that the Recess Clause was "nothing more than a supplement ... for the purpose of establishing an auxiliary method of appointment, in cases to which the general method was inadequate." It would have been improper, he said, to oblige the Senate "to be continually in session for the appointment of officers, and as vacancies might happen *in their recess*, which it might be necessary for the public service to fill without delay, the succeeding clause is evidently intended to authorize the President, *singly*, to make temporary appointments 'during the recess of the Senate, by granting commissions which shall expire at the end of their next session.'"[4] Most of Federalist No. 67 is devoted to rejecting the claim that the President could use the Recess Clause to fill vacancies in the Senate.

Vacancies that "May Happen"

Hamilton's essay raises the question of the meaning of "happen" and "recess." What does the Constitution mean when it refers to vacancies "that may happen during the Recess of the Senate"? Does happen mean "happen to take place" during the recess, as Hamilton suggested? A long list of opinions by Attorneys General has interpreted the language more broadly to mean "happen to exist" at the time of a recess, including vacancies that occur while the Senate is in session and available to give advice and consent. For example, Attorney General Wirt claimed that the second and broader meaning satisfied the reason, scope, and purpose of the Constitution, which to Wirt meant keeping offices filled.[5] Other Attorneys General have reached the same conclusion.[6] In 1880, a federal district court concurred in the position of the Attorney General in opinions issued from 1823 to 1880.[7]

"Recess" of the Senate

The word "recess" also requires interpretation. In 1901, an Attorney General opinion distinguished between the meaning of "adjournment" and "recess" in such a way as to limit *adjournment* to brief periods in the middle of a session, whereas *recess* referred to the period when Congress adjourned at the end of a session. Both words meant the suspension of legislative business, but adjournment implies "a less prolonged intermission than 'recess.'" An adjournment means a "merely temporary suspension of business from day to day, or, when exceeding three days, for such brief periods over holidays as are well recognized and established and as are agreed upon by the joint action of the two Houses." Recess refers to "the period after the final adjournment of Congress for the session, and before the next session begins." Congress "adjourns" in either case, but "[i]t is this period following the final adjournment for the session which is *the recess* during which the President has power to fill vacancies by granting commissions which shall expire at the end of the next session."[8]

The opinion in 1901 said that earlier opinions by Attorneys General on the recess appointment power "relate only to appointments during the recess of the Senate between two sessions of Congress."[9] It acknowledged that if Congress "temporarily adjourned" in the middle of a session "for several months as well as several days," this practice could "seriously curtail the President's power of making recess appointments."[10] Nevertheless, the opinion continued to refer to the interval between one session and the next as "*the* recess."[11]

An Attorney General opinion in 1921 concluded that an adjournment in the middle of a session, from August 24 to September 21, was of sufficient duration to permit recess appointments by the President. Breaking with the 1901 analysis, the Attorney General looked to the "broad and underlying purpose" of the Constitution, which is "to prohibit the President from making appointments without the advice and consent of the Senate whenever that body is in session so that its advice and consent can be obtained." As to whether the Senate "has adjourned or recessed, the real question, as I view it, is whether in a *practical* sense the Senate is in session so that its advice and consent can be obtained. To give the word 'recess' a technical and not a practical construction, is to disregard substance for form."[12]

If a President could make recess appointments during an intrasession adjournment from August 24 to September 21, "does it not necessarily follow that the power exists if an adjournment for only 2 instead of 28 days is taken? I unhesitatingly answer this by saying no."[13] The term "recess" required "a practical construction." When the Senate adjourns for two days, it remains in session. "Nor do I think an adjournment for 5 or even 10 days can be said to constitute the recess intended by the Constitution."[14] In referring to a Senate report written in 1905, the opinion said that the "essential inquiry" consists of these questions: "Is the adjournment of such duration that the members of the Senate owe no duty of attendance? Is its chamber empty? Is the Senate absent so that it can not receive communications from the President or participate as a body in making appointments?"[15]

Subsequent opinions from the Attorney General agreed that significant interruptions in the middle of a session could justify the President's use of the recess appointment power. According to an opinion in 1960, a temporary recess of the Senate, "protracted enough to prevent that body from performing its functions of advising and consenting to executive nominations," permits the President to make recess appointments.[16] Following this interpretation, the Senate's adjournment from July 3 to August 8 in 1960 constituted a "Recess of the Senate."[17]

Opinions by Attorneys General have concluded that short adjournments "for 5 or even 10 days" do not "constitute the recess intended by the Constitution."[18] In 1979, an opinion by the Office of Legal Counsel in the Justice Department held that a recess from August 2 until September 4, 1979, would be of sufficient length to entitle the President to make recess appointments.[19] A Justice Department brief in 1993 suggested that recess appointments might be justified for recesses in excess of three days, but the litigation that prompted this statement was not decided on that ground.[20]

Comptroller General Rulings

The Comptroller General of the General Accounting Office has also offered interpretations of the President's power to make recess appointments. In 1948, the Comptroller General received a letter from the Director of the Administrative Office of the U.S. Courts, regarding the right of payment to four U.S. judges appointed on a recess basis after the Senate adjourned June 20, 1948, to return on December 31, 1948. The Comptroller General cited with approval an earlier Attorney General opinion, which had upheld the use of the President's recess appointment power during an adjournment from August 24 to September 21, 1921.[21] However, the Comptroller General also ruled that one of the judges was not entitled to payment of salary because of a statutory provision that prohibited payment of salary to an individual who had received a recess appointment during a previous recess of the Senate.[22]

FUNDING LIMITATIONS

The broad reading of the Recess Clause by Attorneys General prompted Congress to invoke its power of the purse to limit presidential actions. After Attorneys General had handed down a number of opinions on the power to make recess appointments, Senator William Fessenden remarked in 1863: "It may not be in our power to prevent the [recess] appointment, but it is in our power to prevent the payment; and when payment is prevented, I think that will probably put an end to the habit of making such appointments."[23]

Fessenden made his comment after the Senate had asked its Judiciary Committee to explore this question: Did the practice of appointing officers to fill vacancies that existed *prior* to a recess, while the Senate was in session, conflict with the Constitution? The committee rejected Attorney General Wirt's position that a recess appointee may fill a vacancy that occurs during a session. To the committee, interpreting the constitutional language "may happen during the Recess of the Senate" to include what happened before the recess represented "a perversion of language." Such reasoning, said the committee, tilted political power toward the President and placed undue emphasis on the filling of a vacancy at the expense of Senate prerogatives. Of equal importance to filling vacancies was the need to protect the Senate's opportunity to pass judgment on the qualification of an officeholder. Unless Congress placed some constraint on the President's power to make recess appointments, an "ambitious, corrupt, or tyrannical executive" could nullify the Senate's constitutional function.[24]

Statutory Language in 1863

Congress passed legislation in 1863 to prohibit the use of funds to pay the salary of anyone appointed during a Senate recess to fill a vacancy that existed "while the Senate was in session and is by law required to be filled by and with the advice and consent of the Senate, until such appointee shall have been confirmed by the Senate."[25] Because of this funding restriction, an officer might have to serve without pay (relying on savings or loans) until the Senate consented to the nomination.

That situation arose during the administration of Woodrow Wilson. George Rublee, nominated to the Federal Trade Commission in March 1915, served for more than a year as a recess appointee. After the Senate voted to reject him, he continued to serve the balance of his recess commission until September 1916, when Congress adjourned. Because of the 1863 legislation,

Rublee was not entitled to any remuneration. Congress had to pass a special appropriation to pay his salary for fourteen months: from the date his service began to the date the Senate rejected him.[26]

Revisions in 1940

In 1940, Congress revised the 1863 law to make it less burdensome on officeholders. Congress changed the law to allow for three exceptions in what is now 5 U.S.C. § 5503. As a general rule, payment may not be made to an individual appointed during a Senate recess to fill an existing office if the vacancy existed while the Senate was in session and was by law required to be filled with Senate advice and consent, until the appointee has been confirmed by the Senate.

However, there are three exceptions. First, payments may be made if a vacancy arises within 30 days before the end of the session of the Senate. Given the shortness of time, nominations submitted during that period would be unlikely to gain the Senate's approval. Second, payments may be made if, at the end of the session, a nomination for the office is pending before the Senate (other than for someone appointed during a preceding recess). This provision protects the Senate from successive recess appointees, and it protects nominees whose names go forward in timely manner. Third, payments may be made if a nomination is rejected by the Senate within 30 days before the end of the session and an individual (other than the one rejected) receives a recess appointment. This exception takes care of possible rejections on the eve of a recess. Moreover, the 1940 statute contains an important limitation: A nomination to fill a vacancy referred to in the three exceptions must be submitted to the Senate not later than 40 days after the Senate's next session begins.[27] "Next session" has been interpreted in a nontechnical way to mean the return of the Senate from its recess, not the next session of a Congress.[28]

Dispute in 2001

The application of § 5503 to Article I judges was raised in 2001, after President Clinton made a recess appointment of Sarah L. Wilson to the U.S. Court of Federal Claims. President Clinton nominated her after the 107th Congress convened on January 3, 2001.[29] The Senate then recessed from January 8 to January 20. She was given a recess appointment on January 19 but her nomination was not resubmitted to the Senate, as required under § 5503(b).

Senator Strom Thurmond wrote to the Administrative Office of the U.S. Courts on May 9, stating his belief that Wilson's salary should be suspended because her appointment violated § 5503. He suggested that the Administrative Office request an opinion on the issue from the Office of Personnel Management or the General Accounting Office.[30] William R. Burchill, Jr., Associate Director and General Counsel of the Administrative Office, replied on May 24 that in the opinion of the Administrative Office it was appropriate to pay Judge Wilson's salary and there was no need to seek any outside confirmation of this understanding. Burchill said that Wilson fell within the exception set forth in subsection (a)(2) of § 5503, which states that the salary cutoff shall not apply if, at the end of a session, "a nomination for the office, other than the nomination of an individual appointed during the preceding recess of the Senate, was pending before the Senate for its advice and consent." Wilson's nomination was pending before the Senate when it recessed on January 8.

Burchill agreed that § 5503(b) terminates the entitlement of a recess appointee to pay. However, he said that analyses by the Office of Legal Counsel left it unsettled as to whether the language "next session" in § 5503(b) refers to a post-recess reconvening of the same Congress or the beginning of the session of a Congress that succeeds the adjournment sine die of the current one.[31]

Annual Limitations

In addition to the funding restrictions in § 5503, funding limitations have been included in the annual Treasury-Postal Service appropriations bill. For example, this language appeared in 2000: "No part of any appropriation for the current fiscal year contained in this or any other Act shall be paid to any person for the filling of any position for which he or she has been nominated after the Senate has voted not to approve the nomination of said person."[32]

"Holdover" Provisions

The scope of the recess appointment power can be complicated by the presence of "holdover" clauses in federal statutes. These clauses do not concern the appointment of federal judges, but they have been extensively litigated and help in defining the meaning and application of the Recess Clause. These cases emphasize how Congress, by enacting legislation, can specify when a vacancy exists and expand or limit the President's opportunity to make a recess appointment.

The *Staebler* Case

As an example of a holdover clause, a member of the Federal Election Commission may serve after the expiration of that member's term "until his successor has taken office as a member of the Commission." This type of statutory provision has been litigated because it is unclear how the successor takes office: by Senate confirmation (required for new members) or as a recess appointee. According to the FEC statute, any vacancy in the membership of the commission "shall be filled in the same manner as in the case of the original appointment" (presumably by Senate confirmation). However, on October 25, 1978, President Carter made John McGarry a recess appointee to the seat held by Neil Staebler, who was serving in a holdover capacity. Staebler refused to leave office, arguing that McGarry had not been confirmed by the Senate and therefore no vacancy existed for Carter to fill.

A federal district judge, deciding against Staebler, pointed to some difficulties with the statute. If a vacancy existed only at the point of confirmation for a successor, this might place an unmanageable task on the President. How could he recruit someone for the office and submit a nomination if, in theory, no vacancy existed? The court also concluded that such a result would disrupt the statutory design of staggered, six-year terms for the six commissioners. Following Staebler's interpretation, the statutory dates for these terms might shift to take account of holdovers, creating a "baggage of peculiar practical difficulties."[33] The court could find no clear evidence that Congress had tried to restrict the President's power to make recess appointments.[34] If the Senate wanted to protect its right to advise and consent, it could have rejected McGarry's nomination when Carter first sent it up on September 27, 1977, and again on April 10, 1978. It was only after two years of Senate inaction that Carter made the recess appointment.[35] On appeal, the D.C. Circuit dismissed the case as moot, remanding it to the district court.

Controversies over holdover positions turn on the particular language that Congress enacts. The power to make recess appointments has been a major issue in the life of the Legal Services Corporation (LSC). Through the use of holdover provisions and recess appointments, Presidents Reagan and Bush were able to largely circumvent the Senate's power of confirmation. Several recent court decisions explore the President's power to make recess appointments to the LSC and to other agencies.[36] These decisions analyzed statutory language, such as the length of time the person could remain in holdover status, and whether the holdover "shall" or "may" continue to serve in office. Thus, the scope of the recess appointment power in these areas depends on the particular language that Congress places in a statute.

POLITICAL ACCOMMODATIONS

Confrontations over recess appointments in the 1980s and 1990s led to political agreements between the executive and legislative branches. Although Presidents claimed full constitutional authority to exercise the Recess Clause, they recognized that excessive use of this power could trigger credible threats from Senators to place a hold on all nominations until the White House agreed to an acceptable compromise that satisfied the institutional prerogatives of both branches.

Nomination of Martha Seger

On May 31, 1984, President Reagan nominated Martha R. Seger to be a member of the Board of Governors of the Federal Reserve System.[37] The Senate Banking Committee had held four days of hearings and approved her nomination by the close vote of 10 to 8. A spirited floor debate was expected, but that was foreclosed when Reagan gave her a recess appointment on July 2 after Congress took a three-week break for the Fourth of July holiday (from June 29 to July 23).[38] Senator William Proxmire, chairman of the Banking Committee, accused Reagan of abusing his recess appointment powers and promised to devise remedies that would restrict the President's authority.[39] Lawmakers also objected to other recess appointments made by Reagan.[40]

On August 8, Senator Max Baucus offered an amendment to a supplemental appropriations bills, calling on President Reagan to withdraw the recess appointment for Seger. The Senate voted 53-43 to table the amendment.[41] A day later, Senate Minority Leader Robert C. Byrd introduced a Senate resolution (S.Res. 430), stating that it was the sense of the Senate that the power to make recess appointments should be confined to situations in which the Senate has formally terminated a session or in which the Senate will be in recess for longer than 30 days.[42] That resolution was never put to a vote, but a year later the Senate passed a different resolution offered by Senator Proxmire (S.Res. 194), expressing the sense of the Senate that recess appointments should not be made to the Federal Reserve Board except under unusual circumstances, and only for the purpose of fulfilling "a demonstrable and urgent need" in the administration of the board's activities. The Senate also agreed to consider nominations to the board in an expeditious manner. The resolution was agreed to by voice vote.[43]

On June 13, 1985, the Senate confirmed Seger by voice vote for a term expiring in 1998. On this occasion the Senate Banking Committee voted 11-4 for her confirmation.[44] Although there was controversy over her recess appointment, there was never a question of using a funding restriction to deny appropriated funds for her salary. The Federal Reserve relies on nonappropriated funds to support its operations.

A separate Byrd resolution (S.Res. 213), which the Senate did not act on, stated that the recess appointment power should be confined to a formal termination of a session of the Senate or a recess "protracted enough to prevent it from discharging its constitutional function of advising and consenting to executive nominations." Moreover, it stated that since Presidents and departmental heads were authorized by the Vacancies Act at that time to make temporary appointments for at least 30 days, "no recess appointment should be made when the Senate stands adjourned or recessed within a session for a period of less than thirty days." Finally, the resolution stated that no recess appointment should be made of any person to any office (1) if the person has previously, during the same presidential term, been nominated for appointment to the office, and (2) the Senate has voted not to give its advice and consent to such appointment, or the appropriate committee of the Senate has voted not to report the nomination to the Senate.[45]

Agreement with Senator Byrd

On July 30, 1985, when the Senate was about to recess for the August break, Senator Byrd wrote to President Reagan, stating that the recess should not be considered "the kind of extended recess" contemplated for recess appointments. A broader interpretation, he said, could be seen as "a deliberate effort to circumvent the Constitutional responsibility of the Senate to advise and consent to such appointments."[46] When President Reagan continued to use his recess appointment power broadly, Byrd responded late in 1985 by holding up action on presidential nominations.[47] Senate Majority Leader Bob Dole spoke on September 30 about Byrd's "real concern" about recess appointments and hoped to set up a meeting with the Administration "to allay some of the concerns the distinguished minority leader has."[48] On October 8, the White House announced that President Reagan was "deeply displeased" that Byrd had held up 70 appointments "touching virtually every area of the executive branch," including executive officials and federal judges.[49]

On October 10, a meeting was held in Senator Byrd's office to discuss the problem of recess appointments. In attendance were Senators Dole, Daniel Inouye, Strom Thurmond, and Howard Metzenbaum, plus two officials from the White House, Max Friedersdorf and Fred Fielding. It was agreed that the White House would give notice to the majority and minority leaders prior to a recess, and that the notice would be enough in advance to give the leaders an opportunity to comment on potential recess appointments.[50]

George Mitchell Understanding

On August 4, 1989, Senate Majority Leader George Mitchell warned President George Bush not to give a recess appointment to William Lucas, who had been rejected by the Senate Judiciary Committee to head the Civil Rights Division in the Justice Department. Mitchell argued that the recess appointment power should not be used to sidestep the Senate, and that making a recess appointment of a nominee "who was considered and rejected by the relevant Senate committee . . . would be a very unwise course of action."[51] Lucas did not receive the recess appointment. Instead, Bush named him to be director of the Justice Department's Office of Liaison services, a position that did not require Senate confirmation.[52]

In November 1989, White House Chief of Staff John Sununu suggested that unless the Senate moved more quickly on nominations, President Bush might resort to recess appointments.[53] In a floor statement, Mitchell reiterated the understanding that Senator Byrd had developed on procedures for recess appointments, especially the practice of Presidents notifying party leaders in advance of recess appointments.[54] In 1993, in response to a recess appointment made by President Bush less than two weeks before leaving office, Senator Mitchell placed in the *Congressional Record* an analysis of the recess appointment power prepared by the Senate Legal Counsel. It had been prepared as an amicus brief, to present the Senate's position in a pending recess appointment case, but failed to receive the necessary bipartisan support. The analysis reviewed earlier understandings that the recess appointment power would be utilized "only, and rarely, during substantial intrasession breaks." However, that understanding had now been replaced by the executive branch's claim that "there is no lower time limit" in making recess appointments, a position that "threatens to produce a high level of uncertainty, with regard to appointments, into the relationship between the branches."[55]

Guidelines under Clinton

When the Senate recessed on August 2, 1996, to return on September 3, there was speculation about who President Clinton might appoint on a recess basis. It was considered unlikely that he would make recess appointments of six pending names for federal judgeships: Merrick Garland for the D.C. Circuit, Arthur Gajarsa for the Federal Circuit, William A. Fletcher for the Ninth Circuit, Eric Clay for the Sixth Circuit, and Margaret M. Morrow and Susan McIlway for district court seats. Senate objections would be strong, placing other nominations in jeopardy. Also, the candidates for these federal positions, "especially out-of-towners with families to move, often say they would prefer waiting around for confirmation rather than risk losing the new appointment after little more than a year on the job."[56]

On June 4, 1999, President Clinton issued a recess appointment to James C. Hormel to be ambassador to Luxembourg. The Senate was in recess from May 27 to June 7. When the Senate returned, Senator James Inhofe announced: "I am going to do the same thing Senator Byrd did back in 1985: I am putting holds on every single Presidential nomination."[57] Inhofe charged that Clinton treated the Senate confirmation process "as little more than a nuisance which he can circumvent whenever he wants to impose his will on the country."[58] Inhofe said he would continue to block nominations until Clinton agreed to make them only if Congress was notified in advance and they were "absolutely necessary."[59]

President Clinton had followed the practice of notifying Senate leaders before a recess when he intended to make a recess appointment. In the case of Hormel, however, he did not notify the leaders until June 3, the night before he made the appointment. By that time the Senate had already been in recess for a week.[60] In his response to the Inhofe threat, Clinton wrote to Senator Lott on June 15, stating that his Administration "has made it a practice to notify Senate leaders in advance of our intentions in this regard, and this precedent will continue to be observed."[61] With that agreement in place, Inhofe dropped his threat to block nominations.[62]

The issue flared up again on November 17, 1999, when Senator Inhofe challenged what he considered to be an improper use of the recess appointment power. It was his position that recess appointments "can only be made in the event the vacancy occurs during the recess."[63] A more expansive reading, he said, would magnify executive power at the expense of the Senate prerogative of advice and consent. He reviewed the understanding that Senator Byrd and President Reagan had reached in 1985. Prior to any recess break, the White House would inform the Majority Leader and the Minority Leader of any recess appointment that might be contemplated during the recess. The advance notice would be sufficiently early to allow the leadership on both sides to take action to fill "whatever vacancies that might be imperative during such a break."[64]

President Clinton had agreed to that procedure in his June 15, 1999, letter to Senator Lott, in which he said "I share your opinion that the understanding reached in 1985 between President Reagan and Senator Byrd cited in your letter remains a fair and constructive framework, which my Administration will follow."[65] If the Administration violated the spirit of the agreement, Inhofe and 15 other Senators advised Clinton by letter that they would place holds on "all judicial nominees."[66]

Senator Inhofe read into the *Congressional Record* the names of 13 people submitted by the White House for appointment.[67] The White House-Senate agreement provided a framework but was not strictly adhered to. Some recess appointments were made of names not on the list, and Senator Inhofe was unable to place a total hold on all judicial nominees.[68] On February 11, 2000, the Senate approved Thomas L. Ambro for the Third Circuit and Joel A. Pisano for a district judgeship.[69]

RECESS APPOINTMENTS OF ARTICLE III JUDGES

In 1789, President George Washington made three recess appointments to the federal district courts.[70] From 1789 to 1799, the recess appointment power was used to appoint nine other individuals to federal courts.[71] All were later confirmed by the Senate, except for John Rutledge, who Washington had made Chief Justice under a recess appointment.

John Rutledge

In 1795, John Jay resigned his position as Chief Justice to assume the office of Governor of New York. On July 1, President Washington wrote to John Rutledge of South Carolina, stating that his commission as Chief Justice would take effect on that day as a recess appointee.[72] Rutledge had served as Associate Justice of the U.S. Supreme Court from 1789 to 1791, but resigned that position to become Chief Justice of the South Carolina Court of Common Pleas.

After having been named Chief Justice as a recess appointee, Rutledge gave an intemperate speech on July 16, 1795, bitterly attacking the Jay Treaty. He called it a surrender of American privileges and a "prostitution of the dearest rights of free men." Calling provisions in the treaty the "grossest absurdities" and "ridiculous and inadmissible," he said it would be better for President Washington to die, much as he loved him, than sign the treaty.[73] The speech prompted reports that Rutledge was insane and "daily sinking into debility of mind and body."[74]

On December 10, 1795, President Washington nominated Rutledge to a full life term as Chief Justice. The Senate defeated the nomination five days later, voting 10 to 14.[75] The debate on the nomination is not included in the *Annals of Congress* or the *Senate Executive Journal.* On December 26, Rutledge attempted to drown himself by jumping off a wharf into Charleston Bay.[76] Two days later he wrote to President Washington, resigning his commission as a recess appointee to the position of Chief Justice. He said he was "convinced by Experience, that it requires a Constitution less broken than mine, to discharge with Punctuality and Satisfaction, the Duties of so important an Office."[77]

Presidents continued to make recess appointments for federal judges. In 1983, as an appendix to a brief filed in the case of *United States* v. *Woodley*, the Justice Department prepared a list of 309 individuals who had received recess appointments to Article III courts.[78]

Eisenhower's Appointments

President Dwight D. Eisenhower placed three men on the Supreme Court after recesses by the Senate: Earl Warren, William J. Brennan, Jr., and Potter Stewart. Warren was appointed on a recess basis on October 2, 1953, Brennan on October 15, 1956, and Stewart on October 14, 1958. All three joined the Court and participated in decisions before the Senate had an opportunity to review their credentials. In each case the Senate later gave its advice and consent, but the experience convinced a number of Senators that the procedure was defective for the Senate as well as for the Court.

An article in the *Stanford Law Review* in 1957 reviewed previous recess appointments to the Supreme Court. Although nine such appointments occurred from 1791 to 1862, 91 years elapsed before the recess appointment of Earl Warren. Moreover, of the nine appointments, only two nominees (John Rutledge in 1795 and Benjamin Curtis in 1851) sat on the Court and participated in decisions before being nominated for a life term.[79] The article discussed a number of problems with recess appointments to the federal courts, including the need for a judge to participate and decide cases while having "one eye over his shoulder on Congress," possibly depriving the litigants of a fair hearing.[80]

Members of the House were also concerned about placing individuals on the courts on a recess basis. In January 1959, the House Committee on the Judiciary released a 40-page report entitled "Recess Appointments of Federal Judges." In transmitting the report, committee chairman Emanuel Celler said that the purpose of lifetime appointments "is to secure independence of mind to our judges." If someone is placed on the court with a recess appointment, that person might "measure his decisions" against the knowledge that the Senate Judiciary Committee will later question those rulings. Moreover, it could be argued that the Constitution "guarantees litigants a trial before lifetime judges."[81]

On May 5, 1959, the Senate confirmed Potter Stewart as a Justice of the Supreme Court by the vote of 70 to 17.[82] During the debate, Senator Philip Hart expressed his concern about passing judgment on a judicial nominee who has already been sitting as a recess appointee. As a member of the Senate Committee on the Judiciary with the responsibility for evaluating judicial nominees, he said that the practice of making interim appointments to the Court and having the appointee take his place on the Court "is one which should cease."[83]

Senate Resolution in 1960

In 1960, Senator Hart introduced S.Res. 334 to discourage Presidents from using recess appointments for Justices of the Supreme Court. The resolution stated that it was the sense of the Senate that this type of recess appointment "is not wholly consistent with the best interests of the Supreme Court, the nominee who may be involved, the litigants before the Court, nor indeed the people of the United States." Such appointments should be avoided "except under unusual and urgent circumstances" and, in all such cases, the appointee should not take his seat on the Court until the Senate had given its advice and consent.[84]

As reported by the Senate Committee on the Judiciary, the resolution spoke about institutional interests, such as the "solemn constitutional tasks" of the Senate giving or withholding advice and consent with respect to nominations made to the Supreme court, and doing so, "if possible, in an atmosphere free from pressures inimical to due deliberations." Nominations for the Court "should be considered only in the light of the qualifications the person brings to the threshold of the office." Although previous Presidents had made recess appointments to the Court, "which actions were unquestionably taken in good faith and with a desire to promote the public interest," those appointments were not made with "a full appreciation of the difficulties thereby caused the members of this body." Finally, there is "inevitably public speculation" about the independence of a Justice serving on a recess basis, forced to sit in judgment on cases prior to Senate confirmation. Such speculation, "however ill founded, is distressing to the Court, to the Justice, to the litigants, and to the Senate of the United States."[85]

As a Senate resolution, Hart's proposal could have no legally binding effect, but it was intended to express the position of the Senate and to guide executive actions. Senator Hart referred to the difficulty under which the Senate operated when asked to pass upon the nomination of someone who had already taken a seat as a Justice of the Supreme Court: "it operates to a very great disadvantage upon the Members of the Senate, and I suggest that if this should develop as a traditional practice, as what should be done always, rather than under unusual circumstances, it would adversely affect the Court."[86]

Jefferson B. Fordham, dean of the University of Pennsylvania Law School, remarked that a recess appointee "is serving under the overhang of Senate consideration of a nomination, which is not in harmony with the constitutional policy of judicial independence."[87] Senator Hart added that disappointed litigants might wonder whether the outcome of their case had been influenced by a judge's recess status. Judicial independence, in his view, could be affected by several factors:

> Either to take a position during his period of probation which would please the President who had appointed him and who could withdraw his name; or to please the Senate, which sooner or later, would either approve or disapprove; or, at the other extreme, conscious of the fact that there would

> be public scrutiny and interpretation of his action in light of whether he was bending to the Senate or to the President, he could rear back and bend the other way in order to prove that he was subservient to neither branch.[88]

Opponents of the resolution argued that the President needs to make recess appointments because of the Court's heavy workload.[89] They regarded the filling of vacancies on the Court during recesses as a constitutional power lodged in the President, and felt the Senate should not attempt to meddle with it.[90] It was noted that the power of the Senate is limited to the time after a Justice is nominated, not before.[91] Some Senators objected that the resolution's language was phrased in ambiguous fashion.[92] Finally, it was objected that the resolution had never been referred to the Justice Department or the Judicial Conference for comment, nor had there been any hearings on the resolution.[93] The resolution, including the preamble, reads as follows:

> Whereas one of the solemn constitutional tasks enjoined upon the Senate is to give or withhold its advice and consent with respect to nominations made to the Supreme Court of the United States, doing so, if possible, in an atmosphere free from pressures inimical to due deliberation; and
> Whereas the nomination of a person to the office of Justice of the Supreme Court should be considered only in the light of the qualifications the person brings to threshold of the office; and
> Whereas Presidents of the United States have from time to time made recess appointments to the Supreme Court, which actions were unquestionably taken in good faith and with a desire to promote the public interest, but without a full appreciation of the difficulties thereby caused the Members of this body; and
> Whereas there is inevitably public speculation on the independence of a Justice serving by recess appointment who sits in judgment upon cases prior to his confirmation by this body, which speculation, however ill founded, is distressing to the Court, to the Justice, to the litigants, and to the Senate of the United States: Now, therefore be it
> *Resolved*, That it is the sense of the Senate that the making of recess appointments to the Supreme Court of the United States may not be wholly consistent with the best interests of the Supreme Court, the nominee who may be involved, the litigants before the Court, nor indeed the people of the United States, and that such appointments, therefore, should not be made except under unusual circumstances and for the purpose of preventing or ending a demonstrable breakdown in the administration of the Court's business.

The Senate passed the resolution 48 to 37, voting largely along party lines.[94] Democrats supported it 48-4, with Republicans opposed 33 to 0. The four Democrats voting against the resolution were Edmund Muskie of

Maine, Frank Lausche of Ohio, John Pastore of Rhode Island, and Albert Gore of Tennessee.[95]

LITIGATION

The constitutionality of recess appointments to the federal bench has been litigated in two cases in federal circuit courts. The Supreme Court has not ruled on the issue. When the two cases reached the Court for review, the Court denied certiorari. One case resulted from an appointment by President Dwight D. Eisenhower in 1955. The other case involved an appointment by President Jimmy Carter in 1980.

The *Allocco* Case

On July 31, 1955, Judge Samuel H. Kaufman retired as U.S. district judge for the Southern District of New York. On August 2, the Senate adjourned for the first session of the 84th Congress. On August 17, President Eisenhower issued a recess appointment to John M. Cashin to fill the vacancy left by Kaufman. Cashin took the oath of office for the recess appointment on September 15. Dominic Allocco was tried before Judge Cashin, found guilty by a jury on October 20, and sentenced to 10 years imprisonment. After the Senate reconvened in January 1956, Cashin was confirmed by the Senate and commissioned as a judge with life tenure. He took the oath of office for the commission on March 9, 1956.

Allocco argued that his sentence should be set aside because Judge Cashin was not constitutionally empowered to preside over the trial. He maintained that (1) the President has no power to appoint "temporary" judges, (2) if the President can make interim appointments of judges, they may not preside over criminal trials, and (3) the President has no power to fill vacancies in the judiciary that arise when the Senate is in session.[96]

The Second Circuit ruled that Judge Cashin was constitutionally empowered to preside over the trial. It noted that the Constitution expressly gives the President power to fill up "all" vacancies and that there are no exceptions for judges, which the petitioner wanted the court to find.[97] Since Article II permits the President to make recess appointments for judges, "it necessarily follows that such judicial officers may exercise the power granted to Article III courts," including criminal trials.[98] As to the charge that Presidents may not use the recess appointment power to fill vacancies that arise while the Senate is in session, the court held that this interpretation "would create Executive paralysis and do violence to the orderly functioning of our complex government."[99] The one law review article written in response to this decision was critical of the court's analysis.[100]

The *Woodley* Case

President Carter nominated Walter Heen for a district judgeship in Hawaii on February 28, 1980. On September 25, the Senate Judiciary Committee began confirmation hearings, but no vote had been taken when the Senate recessed on December 16 at the end of the 96th Congress. On December 31, while the Senate was in recess, Carter made Heen a recess appointee. Carter's action came almost two months after he lost to Ronald Reagan. A month after the recess appointment, on January 21, 1981, President Reagan withdrew Heen's nomination and he continued to sit as a district judge until December 16, 1981, when the first session of the 97th Congress ended.

While Judge Heen sat as a recess appointee, Janet Woodley was indicted on a drug charge and filed motions to suppress evidence allegedly obtained in violation of the Fourth Amendment. On November 16, 1981, Judge Heen denied the suppression motions and presided over a trial at which Woodley was found guilty. Woodley challenged Heen's authority to decide these matters as a recess appointee.

In 1983, a three-judge panel of the Ninth Circuit decided this case by analyzing the inherent tension between the President's Article II recess appointment powers and the attributes of judicial independence incorporated into Article III. It held that "only those judges enjoying article III protections may exercise the judicial power of the United States."[101] Only an "even more explicit constitutional provision" could override the values in Article III, and the general language of the recess appointment clause, which "does not mention the judicial branch at all," was insufficient to overcome the command of Article III.[102] The court's review of the records and writings of the constitutional period highlighted the importance of judicial independence to the framers.[103] It also noted that decisions by the Supreme Court have emphasized the importance of an independent judiciary.[104]

The Justice Department argued that the "long and accepted" practice of the President making recess appointments to Article III courts had created an "historical consensus." The court acknowledged that there had been 283 previous recess appointments to the federal bench—six of them to the Supreme Court—and yet also stated that the practice "fell into disuse a generation ago." Judge Heen's appointment in 1980 "was the only recess appointment in the past twenty years."[105] Although both the legislative and executive branches had long accepted the President's power to make recess appointments to the federal bench, and officials in the two branches swear to uphold the Constitution, "the courts alone are the final arbiters of its meaning."[106]

The Ninth Circuit reviewed a number of decisions that had given great weight to historical practice and the constitutional interpretations reached by the political branches. However, it said that that line of reasoning no longer "represents the thinking of the Court," especially after *INS* v. *Chadha* (1983) struck down a 50-year experiment with the legislative veto.[107] Following the reasoning in *Chadha,* which ruled that convenience and efficiency were subordinate values to constitutional commands, the court concluded that to whatever degree recess appointments to judgeships contribute to judicial efficiency, they "offend the explicit and unambiguous command of article III that the judicial power be exercised only by those enjoying life tenure and protection against diminution of compensation."[108]

A majority of the Ninth Circuit voted to rehear the case en banc.[109] In 1985, the full court held that the President may constitutionally confer temporary federal judicial commissions during a recess of the Senate. Judge Heen could therefore constitutionally preside over a criminal trial. The court, divided 7 to 4, decided that there is "no reason to favor one Article over the other."[110] Article II explicitly gave the President the power the fill "all" vacancies during a Senate recess, and there was "no basis upon which to carve out an exception from the recess power for federal judges."[111] The court noted that Presidents had made approximately 300 judicial recess appointments and that Congress "has consistently confirmed judicial recess appointees without dissent."[112] The court further noted that Rutledge was not confirmed, but the Senate rejected him not because he was a recess appointee but because of his speeches against the Jay Treaty.[113]

As to the importance of *Chadha*, the court noted that the legislative veto is "a recent practice, barely 50 years old," whereas recess appointments to federal courts "reach back to the days of the Framers."[114] Considerable weight is given to unbroken practices "acquiesced in by the Framers of the Constitution when they were participating in public affairs."[115] Since a recess appointee lacks life tenure and is not protected by salary diminution, the individual "is in theory subject to greater political pressure than a judge whose nomination has been confirmed."[116] However, "[e]ven viewing the recess clause as an unwise constitutional provision, it is not for this court to redraft the Constitution. Changes in that great document must come through constitutional amendment, not through judicial reform based on policy arguments."[117]

Judge Heen served out his recess appointment, which lasted until the end of the first session of the 97th Congress. President Reagan did not nominate him to a lifetime appointment. Heen left the federal court to sit on the Hawaii State Intermediary Court of Appeals.[118] Because of Carter's defeat by Reagan, Heen said he knew his service on the federal bench would be short-term. He concluded that the recess appointment in his case was "an exercise in futility [because] you know you're not going to be around."[119]

Four law review articles analyzed the *Woodley* case. Two of the articles, responding to the panel decision, argued that recess appointments to federal courts are a valid exception to the Article III requirements for life tenure and no-diminution.[120] The other two, written after the en banc ruling, concluded that recess appointments to the federal judiciary contravene Article III requirements and argued that recess appointees may not exercise Article III powers.[121]

However one analyzes the decision of the Ninth Circuit, sitting en banc, it stands only for the proposition that if the President and the Senate agree to recess appointments for federal courts, the appointments are not constitutionally invalid. The decision does not mean that the President and the Senate are forced in any way to accept recess appointments to federal courts as the preferred or even acceptable course. The two political branches could decide, on either political or constitutional grounds, that the recess appointment power should not be applied to the judiciary.

Gregory's Appointment

On the last day of the 106th Congress, December 15, 2000, with the Senate about to adjourn sine die, Senate Majority Leader Trent Lott voiced concern about the President's use of recess appointments, "especially appointments to the Federal judiciary."[122] Senator Byrd cautioned that the Recess Clause "is not put in there to enable any President, Republican or Democrat, to play games with the Senate, or to attempt to do a one-upmanship simply because the Senate is out of session." He said he "especially hope[d]" that the Administration would not attempt "to fill a Federal judgeship during the recess of the Senate," and that he would not support "any administration, Democratic or Republican, that attempts to fill Federal judgeships while the Senate is in recess." Lott added that he had not been notified of any recess appointments "or any Federal judicial appointment during this recess period." He agreed with Byrd that "any appointment of a Federal judge during a recess should be opposed." In recalling the Eisenhower recess appointments to the federal courts, Lott said that "was a mistake then, and it would be one now."[123]

President Clinton had nominated Roger L. Gregory to the Fourth Circuit on June 30, 2000.[124] On December 27, he announced Gregory's recess appointment, the first time since 1980 that a President had named an Article III judge as a recess appointee. Clinton offered several reasons for his decision. He said that the U.S. Judicial Conference had declared the seat "a judicial emergency" and that it had been vacant for more than a decade. He regarded it as "unconscionable that the fourth circuit, with the largest African-American population of any circuit in our Nation, has never had an African-American appellate judge." Having offered nominations in the past for this vacancy, without obtaining confirmation from the Senate, he decided that a recess appointment was justified.[125] Clinton said he had "tried for 5 years to put an African-American on the fourth circuit."[126]

Press reports put the Gregory recess appointment in a larger context. Newspaper accounts described efforts by the Clinton White House to "put the Senate's record on black judges in play in the midst of controversy over President-elect Bush's attorney general nominee, Sen. John D. Ashcroft, who has been roundly condemned by civil rights groups for torpedoing the nomination of another African American judicial candidate, Missouri Supreme Court Justice Ronnie White."[127] Other reports suggest that the decision to put Gregory on the court as a recess appointee was made before Election Day.[128] Rep. James E. Clyburn, chairman of the Congressional Black Caucus, stated that if Senate Republicans tried to remove Gregory, racial representation on the federal bench "would be an even bigger issue in the mid-term elections than it already is."[129] Another news story interpreted the recess appointment as not only placing the first black on the Fourth Circuit but "one also carefully calculated to create political difficulties for the Republican Party."[130]

Senator Inhofe, announcing that he would block any effort to confirm Gregory for a lifetime appointment, called it "outrageously inappropriate for any president to fill a federal judgeship through a recess appointment in a deliberate way to bypass the Senate."[131] It was reported that Senator Lott had told Clinton he would oppose any recess appointments of judges.[132]

On January 3, 2001, President Clinton renominated Gregory for the 107th Congress.[133] On March 19, President George W. Bush withdrew the names of 10 nominees for federal judgeships, including Gregory.[134] In the meantime, the Senate and the White House negotiated over the procedures for acting on judicial nominees. By early May, it was reported that Senate Democrats said they would not agree to confirmation votes for Theodore B. Olson as Solicitor General and Larry Thompson as Deputy Attorney General unless the Republicans restored the right of individual Senators to block judicial nominations from their home states. They also said they would block action on any judicial nomination until the issue was resolved.[135] In what was interpreted as a conciliatory move, President Bush announced eleven nominations for the federal judiciary on May 9, including the name of Roger Gregory for a lifetime appointment to the Fourth Circuit.[136]

The Senate Judiciary Committee cleared Gregory on July 19 by a vote of 19 to 0.[137] On the following day, the Senate approved Gregory 93 to 1, the sole negative vote coming from Senator Lott.[138] Although there was no floor statement by Senator Lott, the media quoted his spokesman saying that his opposition to Gregory was "an institutional decision" designed to protect Senate prerogatives and emphasize his position that "any appointment of federal judges during a recess should be opposed."[139] During the floor debate, Senator George Allen spoke in favor of Gregory but did not want his support interpreted as condoning "the former President's political manipulations" and the "past procedural aggravation."[140]

CONCLUSIONS

Despite litigation in *Allocco* and *Woodley*, the President's use of recess appointments for federal judges remains an unsettled constitutional issue. The President's appointment powers under Article II are in tension with the Senate's confirmation role and with the constitutional guarantees to federal judges under Article III. The issues identified by Senator Hart in his 1960 resolution are still with us. Individuals placed on Article III courts for an interim period lack the independence of judges who are given life tenure and are protected against diminution of salary. Recess appointees weaken the advice and consent role of the Senate and, some believe, diminish the constitutional protections accorded to litigants.

As a result of the controversy over the Eisenhower recess appointments of Warren, Brennan, and Stewart, there appears to be a political agreement that the President should not use recess appointment powers for Justices of the Supreme Court. After President Carter's appointment of Judge Heen, there seemed to be a similar agreement for lower court judges. Because of President Clinton's appointment of Judge Gregory, the dispute over recess appointments for district courts and the federal circuits has been rekindled.

The Senate can issue sense-of-the-Senate resolutions and other non-binding statements, but it cannot prevent the President from invoking the recess appointment power to appoint federal judges. However, the issue is as much subject to political checks and understandings as it is to judicial rulings. The Senate always has the option of making it clear that such interim appointments would be defeated overwhelmingly when the individual is nominated for a lifetime appointment. Should it do so, it would give notice that such appointees could expect limited tenure. Presidents would then decide whether it is worth the laborious process of completing background checks on nominees and interviewing them, merely to put judges on the court for brief periods.

References

[1] U.S. Const. art. II, § 2, cl. 3.

[2] 2 *The Records of the Federal Convention of 1787,* at 540, 574, 600, 660 (New Haven: Yale University Press, 1937, Max Farrand ed.) (hereafter "Farrand"); 3 Farrand 421.

[3] *The Federalist*, by Alexander Hamilton, James Madison, and John Jay 436-440 (Cambridge, Mass.: Harvard University Press, 1961, Benjamin Fletcher Wright ed.).

[4] Id. at 438-39 (emphasis in original).

[5] 1 Op. Att'y Gen. 631 (1823).

[6] 2 Op. Att'y Gen. 525 (1832); 4 Op. Att'y Gen. 523 (1846); 10 Op. Att'y Gen. 356 (1862); 12 Op. Att'y Gen. 32, 38 (1866); 12 Op. Att'y Gen. 455, 457 (1868); 16 Op. Att'y Gen. 522, 524 (1880); 18 Op. Att'y Gen. 29 (1884); 19 Op. Att'y Gen. 261, 262 (1889); 30 Op. Att'y Gen. 314, 315 (1914); 33 Op. Att'y Gen. 20, 23 (1921); 41 Op. Att'y Gen. 463, 465-66 (1960).

[7] In re Farrow, 3 F. 112, 113-15 (C.C. N.D. Ga. 1880).

[8] 23 Op. Att'y Gen. 599, 601 (1901) (emphasis in original).

[9] Id. at 602.

[10] Id. at 603.

[11] Id. at 604 (emphasis in original).

[12] 33 Op. Att'y Gen. 20, 21-22 (1921) (emphasis in original).
[13] Id. at 24.
[14] Id. at 25.
[15] Id.
[16] 41 Op. Att'y Gen. 463, 466 (1960).
[17] Id.
[18] 33 Op. Att'y Gen. 20, 25 (1921).
[19] 3 Op. Off. Legal Counsel 314 (1979).
[20] Memorandum of Points and Authorities in Support of Defendants' Opposition to Plaintiffs' Motion for Partial Summary Judgment, at 24-26, Mackie v. Clinton, Civ. Action No. 93-0032-LFO (D.D.C.).
[21] 28 Comp. Gen. 30, 34-37 (1948).
[22] Id. at 37-38.
[23] Cong. Globe, 37th Cong., 3rd sess. 565 (1863).
[24] S. Rept. No. 80, 37th Cong., 3rd sess. 5-6 (1863).
[25] 12 Stat. 646 (1863).
[26] 39 Stat. 801 (1916).
[27] 54 Stat. 751 (1950); 5 U.S.C. § 5503 (1994).
[28] 41 Op. Att'y Gen. 463, 477 (1960)
[29] 37 Weekly Comp. Pres. Doc. 105 (2001).
[30] Letter from Senator Strom Thurmond to the Honorable Leonidas Ralph Mecham, Director, Administrative Office of the U.S. Courts, May 9, 2001.
[31] Letter from William R. Burchill, Jr., Associate Director and General Counsel of the Administrative Office of the U.S. Courts to Senator Strom Thurmond, May 24, 2001, at 2.
[32] 114 Stat. 2763A-157, § 609 (2000).
[33] Staebler v. Carter, 464 F.Supp. 585, 589 (D.D.C. 1979).
[34] Id. at 592.
[35] Id. at 601. For the Senate's record on McGarry, see id. at 587.
[36] Swan v. Clinton, 100 F.3d 973 (D.C. Cir. 1996); Wilkinson v. Legal Services Corp., 865 F.Supp. 891 (D.D.C. 1994), reversed on other grounds, Wilkinson v. Legal Services Corp., 80 F.3d 535 (D.C.Cir. 1996); Mackie v. Clinton, 827 F.Supp. 56 (D.D.C. 1993); McCalpin v. Durant, 766 F.2d 535 (D.C. Cir. 1985); McCalpin v. Dana, No. 85-542 (D.D.C. 1982). See "An LSC Dispute May Take Power from President," National Law Journal, February 19, 1996, at A1.
[37] Public Papers of the Presidents, 1984, II, at 777.
[38] Id. at 1915.

[39] "Proxmire: Seger Appointment Cut Constitutional Corners," *Washington Post*, July 6, 1984, at D3.
[40] "Reagan's Recess Hirings Elicit Resentment," *Washington Post*, July 11, 1984, at A17; "Reagan's Recess Appointments Rankle Hill," *Washington Post*, July 14, 1984, at 1698.
[41] 130 Cong. Rec. 22767-82 (1984).
[42] Id. at 23234-36, 23341.
[43] 131 Cong. Rec. 17622-24, 17679 (1985).
[44] 1985 CQ Almanac 420.
[45] Id. at 22419, 22496-97.
[46] Id. at 22498.
[47] "Recess Appointments Raise Senators' Anger," *Washington Post*, September 26, 1985, at A23; Public Papers of the Presidents, 1985 (II), at 1209; "White House Asks End of Appointee 'Backlog,'" *Washington Post*, October 9, 1985, at A17.
[48] 131 Cong. Rec. 25303 (1985).
[49] Public Papers of the Presidents, 1985, II, at 1209; "White House Asks End to Appointee 'Backlog,'" *Washington Post*, October 9, 1985, at A17.
[50] 131 Cong. Rec. 27312-13, 27686-87 (1985).
[51] "Mitchell Opposes Recess Appointment," *Washington Post*, August 5, 1989, at A5.
[52] 1989 CQ Almanac 31.
[53] "Senate Pressed on Nominees," *Washington Post*, November 11, 1989, at A25.
[54] 135 Cong. Rec. 28390, 31445-46 (1989); "Mitchell Cautions On Appointments," *Washington Post*, November 15, 1989, at A19.
[55] 139 Cong. Rec. 15267 (1993). See "Recess Appointments: A Disputed Matter of Timing," *Washington Post*, July 19, 1993, at A13.
[56] "The Recess Appointment Game," *Washington Post*, August 12, 1996, at A11.
[57] 145 Cong. Rec. S6654 (daily ed. June 8, 1999).
[58] "Choice of Hormel Spurs Vow to Block Nominees," *Washington Post*, June 9, 1999, at A23.
[59] "In Protest of Clinton Action, Senator Blocks Nominations," *New York Times*, June 9, 1999, at A20.
[60] "Clinton Vow to Congress Ends a Threat to His Nominations," *New York Times*, June 17, 1999, at A22.
[61] Id.

[62] "Inhofe Ends Threat to Clinton Nominees," *Washington Post*, June 17, 1999, at A17.

[63] 145 Cong. Rec. S14665 (daily ed. November 17, 1999).

[64] Id.

[65] Id. at S14666.

[66] Id. The Senators signing the letter included Jesse Helms, Wayne Allard, Michael Crapo, Michael B. Enzi, Bob Smith, George Voinovich, Pete B. Domenici, James M. Inhofe, Phil Gramm, Mitch McConnell, Craig Thomas, Rod Grams, Tim Hutchinson, Conrad Burns, Chuck Grassley, and Richard Shelby.

[67] Id. at S15060 (daily ed. November 19, 1999).

[68] "Recess appointee wasn't on list," Washington Times, December 22, 1999, at A1; "Senator Vows to Stall Action on Judgeships," *New York Times*, December 21, 1999, at A22; 146 Cong. Rec. S582-84 (daily ed. February 10, 2000); CRS Report RL30821, "Recess Appointments Made by President Clinton," by Rogelio Garcia (January 26, 2001).

[69] 146 Cong. Rec. S584–89 (February 10, 2000); "Lott Overrides 'Holds': Two Judges Confirmed," *Washington Post*, February 11, 2000, at A4.

[70] 30 The Writings of George Washington 457-58, 473, 485 n.75 (Washington, D.C.: Government Printing Office, 1940).

[71] Robert Morris, recess appointment of August 28, 1790; William Lewis, July 14, 1791; Thomas Johnson, August 5, 1791; Samuel Hitchcock, September 3, 1793; John Rutledge, July 1, 1795; Joseph Clay, Jr., September 16, 1796; Benjamin Bourne, October 13, 1796; Bushrod Washington, September 29, 1798; James Winchester, October 1, 1799 (Second Supplemental Brief for the United States, United States v. Woodley, No. 82-1028, Ninth Circuit, 1983, at A1-A25).

[72] 34 *The Writings of George Washington 225*. The temporary commission is reprinted in 1 Documentary History of the Supreme Court of the United States, 1789-1800, at 96 (New York: Columbia University Press, 1985, Maeva Marcus and James R. Perry, eds.).

[73] Leon Friedman, "John Rutledge," in 1 The Justices of the United States Supreme Court, 1789-1969, at 45 (New York: Chelsea House Publishers, 1969).

[74] Id. at 46.

[75] 1 Journal of the Executive Proceedings of the Senate 195-96.

[76] Friedman, "John Rutledge," at 48.

[77] 1 Documentary History of the Supreme Court 100.

[78] Second Supplemental Brief for the United States, United States v. Woodley, No. 82-1028, Ninth Circuit, at A1-A25.
[79] "Recess Appointments to the Supreme Court—Constitutional But Unwise?," 10 Stan. L. Rev. 124, 125, 131 (1957).
[80] Id. at 144.
[81] "Recess Appointments of Federal Judges," House Committee on the Judiciary, 86th Cong., 1st sess. iii (Comm. Print, January 1959).
[82] 105 Cong. Rec. 7472 (1959).
[83] Id. at 7467.
[84] 106 Cong. Rec. 12761 (1960).
[85] S. Rept. No. 1893, 86th Cong., 2nd sess. 1-2 (1960).
[86] 106 Cong. Rec. 18131 (1960).
[87] Id. at 18132.
[88] Id. at 18134.
[89] Id. at 18133 (Senator Hruska).
[90] Id. at 18134 (Senator Wiley).
[91] Id. at 18135 (Senator Wiley).
[92] Id.
[93] Id. at 18137 (Senator Hruska).
[94] Id. at 18145.
[95] 1960 CQ Almanac, at 517.
[96] United States v. Allocco, 305 F.2d 704, 706 (2d Cir. 1962), cert. denied, 371 U.S. 964 (1963).
[97] Id. at 708-09.
[98] Id. at 709.
[99] Id. at 712.
[100] John S. Castellano, "A New Look at Recess Appointments to the Federal Judiciary—*United States v. Allocco*," 12 Cath. U. L. Rev. 29 (1963).
[101] United States v. Woodley, 726 F.2d 1328, 1330 (9th Cir. 1983).
[102] Id. at 1331.
[103] Id. at 1331-32.
[104] Id. at 1334-35.
[105] Id. at 1336.
[106] Id.
[107] Id. at 1337.
[108] Id. at 1338.
[109] United States v. Woodley, 732 F.2d 111 (9th Cir. 1984).
[110] United States v. Woodley, 751 F.2d 1008, 1010 (9th Cir. 1985), cert. denied, 475 U.S. 1048 (1986).

[111] Id.
[112] Id. at 1011.
[113] Id. at 1010, n.5.
[114] Id. at 1011.
[115] Id. at 1012.
[116] Id. at 1014.
[117] Id.
[118] "U.S. Judge's Recess Appointment Ruled Illegal," *National Law Journal,* December 26, 1983, at 15.
[119] "Recess Appointee Says It's Not a Great Idea," *Washington Post*, November 8, 1999, at A19.
[120] Thomas A. Curtis, "Recess Appointments to Article III Courts: The Use of Historical Practice in Constitutional Interpretation," 84 Colum. L. Rev. 1758 (1984); Joann Gaona, "Recess Appointment Power—Exception to or Violation of Article III," 1984 Ariz. St. L. J. 783 (1984).
[121] Paul Ferris Solomon, "Answering the Unasked Question: Can Recess Appointees Constitutionally Exercise the Judicial Power of the United States?," 54 Cinc. L. Rev. 631 (1985); Virginia L. Richards, "Temporary Appointments to the Federal Judiciary: Article II Judges?," 60 N.Y.U. L. Rev. 702 (1985).
[122] 146 Cong. Rec. S11833 (daily ed. December 15, 2000).
[123] Id. at S11834.
[124] 36 Weekly Comp. Pres. Doc. 1564 (2000).
[125] Id. at 3180.
[126] Id. at 3182.
[127] "Clinton Names Black Judge to Appeals Court," *Washington Post*, December 28, 2000, at A8.
[128] "4th Circuit Surprise," *Legal Times*, January 1, 2001, at 6.
[129] "Clinton Names Black Judge to Appeals Court," *Washington Post*, December 28, 2000, at A8.
[130] "Clinton Names A Black Judge; Skirts Congress," *New York Times*, December 28, 2000, at A1.
[131] "Senator Vows He Will Fight Clinton's Judicial Selection," *New York Times*, December 29, 2000, at A15.
[132] Id.
[133] 37 Weekly Comp. Pres. Doc. 4-5 (2001).
[134] 37 Weekly Comp. Pres. Doc. 503 (2001); "ABA's Role in Vetting U.S. Judges Is Reviewed," *Washington Post*, March 20, 2001, at A1.

[135] "Democrats Block Picks for 2 Justice Posts," *Washington Post*, May 4, 2001, at A10.
[136] 37 Weekly Comp. Pres. Doc. 724-25 (2001); "Bush Will Nominate 11 as U.S. Judges," *Washington Post*, Mary 9, 2001, at A1.
[137] "Panel Clears Judge Gregory, Two Others," *Washington Post,* July 20, 2001, at A2.
[138] 147 *Cong. Rec.* S7992 (daily ed. July 20, 2001).
[139] "Senators Confirm 3 Judges, Including Once-Stalled Black," *New York Times*, July 21, 2001, at A28.
[140] 147 *Cong. Rec.* S7991 (daily ed. July 20, 2001).

SELECTED BIBLIOGRAPHY

Carrier, Michael A. "When Is the Senate in Recess for Purposes of the Recess Appointments Clause?," 92 *Michigan Law Review* 2204 (1994).

Castellano, John S. "A New Look at Recess Appointments to the Federal Judiciary—*United States v. Allocco*," 12 *Catholic University Law Review* 29 (1963).

Chanen, Stuart J. "Constitutional Restrictions on the President's Power to Make Recess Appointments," 79 *Northwestern University Law Review* 191 (1984).

Curtiss, Thomas A. "Recess Appointments to Article III Courts: The Use of Historical Practice in Constitutional Interpretation," 84 *Columbia Law Review* 1758 (1984).

Gaona, Joann. "Federal Courts—Recess Appointment Power—Exception to or Violation of Article II," 1984 *Arizona State Law Journal* 783 (1984).

Note. "Recess Appointments to the Supreme Court—Constitutional But Unwise?," 10 *Stanford Law Review* 124 (1957).

Richards, Virginia L. "Temporary Appointments to the Federal Judiciary: Article II Judges?," 60 *New York University Law Review* 702 (1985).

Solomon, Paul Ferris. "Answering the Unasked Question: Can Recess Appointees Constitutionally Exercise the Judicial Power of the United States?," 54 *Cincinnati Law Review* 631 (1985).

U.S. Congress. House Committee on the Judiciary, "Recess Appointments of Federal Judges," 86th Cong., 1st sess. (*Committee Print*, January 1959).

——. Senate Committee on the Judiciary, "Expressing the Sense of the Senate that Recess Appointments to the Supreme Court of the United States Should Not Be Made Except Under Unusual Circumstances," S. Rept. No. 1893, 86th Cong., 2nd sess. (1960).

——. Subcommittee on General Oversight and Investigations of the House Committee on Banking and Financial Services, "The Termination of Mr. Robert H. Swan as a Member of the Board of the National Credit Union Administration," 104th Cong., 2nd sess. (1996).

INDEX

A

B

C

D

E

F

G

H

I

J

L

M

P

Q

R

S

T

U

V

W